ABOUT BATESON

Books by John Brockman

As Author
By the Late John Brockman
37
Afterwords

As Coauthor
The Philosopher's Game

As Editor
Real Time 1
Real Time 2

ABOUT BATESON

❁ ❁

Essays on Gregory Bateson by:

Mary Catherine Bateson
Ray Birdwhistell
John Brockman
David Lipset
Rollo May
Margaret Mead
Edwin Schlossberg

Afterword by Gregory Bateson

Edited by John Brockman

WILDWOOD HOUSE • London

First published in Great Britain 1978

ISBN: 0–7045–0325–5

Designed by Ann Gold

CONTENTS

Introduction

❂ ❂

JOHN BROCKMAN

It is March 1973 in Big Sur, California. A diverse group of thinkers are assembled to spend ten days together exploring the work of British mathematician G. Spencer Brown. Alan Watts and John Lilly, the coorganizers, are billing the event as "The AUM Conference," shorthand for The American University of Masters.

They have gathered together intellectuals, philosophers, psychologists, and scientists. Each has been asked to lecture on his own work in terms of its relationship to Brown's new ideas in mathematics. G. Spencer Brown lectures for two days on his *Laws of Form.* Alan Watts talks of Eastern religious thought. John Lilly discusses maps of reality. Karl Pribram explores new possibilities for thinking about neuroscience. Ram Dass presents a spiritual path. Stewart Brand lectures on whole systems. Psychologists Will Schutz, Claudio Naranjo, and Charles Tart are in attendance. Heinz von Foerster holds forth on cybernetic modeling. My own topic is "Einstein, Gertrude Stein, Wittgenstein, and Frankenstein."

Perhaps, of all the "Masters" present, Gregory Bateson, at sixty-eight, is at once the best known and the least known. Among his assembled peers, his reputation is formidable. At the AUM Conference, stories of his profound effect on postmodern thinking abound. Yet few outside the relatively small circle of avant-garde thinkers know about him or his work.

There is valid reason. Bateson is not very accessible. His major book, *Steps to an Ecology of Mind,* is just being published. It is a collection of essays he has written over a thirty-five-year period.

Bateson begins lecturing in the conference room. Clearly he is held in awe by his colleagues. Nothing in his imposing presence detracts from his reputation. He is a large man with a deep rich voice imbued with an unmistakable English accent. There is an air of authenticity about him.

His talk is filled with brilliant insights and vast erudition as he takes us on a tour of subjects that include zoology, psychiatry, anthropology, aesthetics, linguistics, evolution, cybernetics, and epistemology. "The point," he says, "is that the ways of nineteenth-century thinking are becoming rapidly bankrupt, and new ways are growing out of cybernetics, systems theory, ecology, meditation, psychoanalysis, and psychedelic experience."

As he talks I look through a paper he has left for us as we entered the room. "Form, Substance, and Difference" is the nineteenth Korzybski Lecture, delivered by Bateson in 1970. In it he points out that he's touched on numerous fields but is an expert in none. He's not a philosopher, nor is anthropology exactly his business. This doesn't help me much. All I know about him is that he has an anthropological background, was once married to Margaret Mead, and was a prime mover behind the important Macy Conferences in Cybernetics in the 1940s.

His theme in the Korzybski Lecture was the same as his theme today: "the area of impact between very abstract and formal philosophic thought on the one hand and the natural history of man and other creatures on the other." His ideas are clearly of an epistemological nature. He asks us to do away with our Newtonian language, our Cartesian coordinates, to see the world in terms of the mind we all share. Bateson presents a new approach based on a cybernetic epistemology: "The individual mind is immanent but not only in the body. It is immanent also in the pathways and messages outside the body; and there is a larger mind of which the individual mind is only a subsystem. This larger mind is comparable to God and is perhaps what some people mean by 'God,' but it is still immanent in the total interconnected social system and planetary ecology."

"Very few people have any idea of what I am talking about," Bateson says as he picks at a piece of fish in a Malibu restaurant. We are having dinner and discussing his plans for a new book concerning evolutionary theory. It is June 1973. (At the AUM Conference in March, I had been pressed into service as a literary agent.)

Bateson defies simple labeling, easy explanation. People have problems with his work. He talks of being an explorer who cannot know what he is exploring until it has been explored. His introduction to *Steps* states: "I found that in my work with primitive peoples, schizophrenia, biological symmetry, and in my discontent with the conventional theories of evolution and learning, I had identified a widely scattered set of bench marks as points of reference from which a new scientific territory could be defined. These bench marks I have called 'Steps' in the title of the book."

But this is where Bateson gets difficult. Just what is this "new scientific territory"? Most people look for the next place, the next piece of knowledge. Instead, Bateson presents an epistemology so radical that as one climbs from step to step, the ground supporting the ladder abruptly vanishes. Not easy, this cybernetic explanation of Gregory Bateson. Not comfortable. Not supportive. Not loving. The center dissolves, and man is dead; and in his place we have the metaphysical I. So dismiss yourself; let go: There's nothing lost.

Bateson's readers often find it difficult to grasp that his way of thinking is different from theirs. His students believe that he is hiding something from them, that there's a secret behind his thinking that he won't share. There's something to this. Bateson is not clearly understood because his work is not an explanation, but a commission. As Wittgenstein noted, "a commission tells us what we must do." In Bateson's case, what we must do is reprogram ourselves, train our intelligence and imagination to work according to radical configurations. Heinz Von Foerster points out that "the blessed curse of a metalanguage is that it wears the cloth of a first-order language, an 'object language.' Thus, any proposition carries with it the tantalizing ambiguity: Was it made in meta or in object language?" Nobody knows and you can't find out. All attempts to speak *about* a metalanguage, that is, to speak *in* meta-metalanguage, are doomed to fail. As Wittgenstein observed: "Remain silent!" But Bateson cannot remain silent. His childlike curiosity, his intellectual vigor and strength compel him to continue exploring new ground.

Yet he is hesitant about writing his new book. *The Evolutionary Idea* will be the first major restatement of evolutionary theory in half a century. Based on his previous experience, he is worried about the difficulty of getting across his ideas. The implications of the theory are based on acceptance of a radical new order of things, a worldview totally alien to our traditional Western way of thinking.

"Evolutionists are an anxious, conservative, and spiteful bunch," he says. "In fact, they kill each other." Bateson is referring to the famous affair involving his father, William Bateson, and William Kammerer, the Austrian biologist. Kammerer, a Lamarckian, committed suicide over research involving the inherited characteristics of the midwife toad. "I don't think they will like this book very much," Bateson says, realizing that he will be straying far from the traditional debate of natural selection versus inherited characteristics.

Bateson contends that as a result of advances in cybernetics and fundamental mathematics, many other areas of thought have shifted. In *The Evolutionary Idea,* he will gather together these new advances to present an alternative to current orthodox theories of evolution. This alternative view will stress the role of *information,* that is, of *mind,* in all levels of biology from genetics to ecology and from human culture to the pathology of schizophrenia. In place of natural selection of organisms, Bateson will consider the survival of patterns, ideas, and forms of interaction.

"Any descriptive proposition," he says, "which remains true longer will out-survive other propositions which do not survive so long. This switch from the survival of the creatures to the survival of ideas which are immanent in the creatures (in their anatomical forms and in their interrelationships) gives a totally new slant to evolutionary ethics and philosophy. Adaptation, purpose, homology, somatic change, and mutation all take on new meaning with this shift in theory."

It is the morning after our dinner discussion about the new book. Bateson, about forty other people, and I are together for a two-day seminar to explore "Ecology of Mind." Most of the people have paid one hundred dollars to hear Bateson talk. The auspices are an institute for humanistic development. The audience appears to be interested in self-help and personal awareness. This is the first opportunity I have had to hear him speak before a general audience. After the excitement surrounding his performance at the AUM Conference, I am preparing myself for another memorable experience.

Bateson slowly guides us through his endless repertoire of concepts and ideas. He talks about metaphor versus sacrament, schismogenesis, metaphysics, explanatory principles, heuristic versus fundamental ideas, the value of deduction, steady state society, metapropositions, deuterolearning, cybernetic explanation, idea as difference, logical categories of learning, mental determinism, end linkage, and on and on.

After a few hours, the attention of the group begins to wander. Many appear to be bored. By the end of the first day, at least one-third of the people have left. Bateson is unperturbed. Many people seek him out for the wrong reasons: for entertainment; for answers; as a guru. He explains that his receptions vary from the extreme boredom of this day to the excitement of the Macy Conferences of the 1940s. Still, he is always willing to travel, to interact with all kinds of people in order to present his ideas. "Why do you bother?" I ask in reference to this particularly moribund gathering. It is clear that few here have any inkling of what he is saying. "One simply keeps going," he says gently, "and leaves the name behind."

Christmas time, 1973. I am about to approach a publisher to sell rights to *The Evolutionary Idea.* I had phoned Bateson requesting a biographical sketch. His letter arrives:

"John Brockman suggests that I write you a personal letter telling you who I am. I enclose an outline curriculum vitae,* to which I will add as follows.

"My father was William Bateson, F.R.S., geneticist, a fellow of St. John's College, and first director of the John Innes Horticultural Institute, which was and still is a large genetical research institute.

"Boyhood was mainly devoted to natural history: butterflies and moths, beetles, dragonflies, marine invertebrates, flowering plants, etc.

"Cambridge was mainly biology until I got a chance to go to the Galapagos Islands, where I realized that I did not know what to do with field natural history. In those days, biology, both in field and lab, was mainly taxonomy, and I knew that was not what I wanted to do. So, on return to Cambridge, I took anthropology under A. C. Haddon, who sent me out to the Sepik River, New Guinea, to study historical culture contact between the Sepik and the Fly River peoples. This was the equivalent in anthropology of taxonomy in biology. The result was two field expeditions, groping very unhappily for what one could do to establish some theory in anthropology. The final product was *Naven,* a book which was then very difficult for people to read but is gradually coming into almost orthodoxy. Levi-Strauss has worked on some of the problems of cultural structure which I raised then, and I think he's done

* See page 248 ff.

a good deal to make my stuff readable and 'safe' for anthropologists.

"After that, field work in the Dutch Indies, in Bali, with my wife Margaret Mead. Then I did an elaborate photographic study of personal relations among the Balinese, especially interchange between parents and children. This was published with about 700 photographs as *Balinese Character*.

"Not much of my period of fellowship at St. John's College was spent in Cambridge. I was mostly in New Guinea and Bali. But of course it was an important piece of my life, and there were important people—L. S. B. Leakey, Harold Jeffries, Claude Guillebaud, Reginald Hall, Teulon Porter, Sir Frederick Bartlett, and others.

"In those days I was on the sidelines of the anthropologically famous battles between Radcliffe-Brown and Malinowski. I'd taught under Radcliffe-Brown in Sydney and learned a great deal from him, some of which got built into *Naven* (the hook-up with French anthropology came down to me from Durkheim and Mauss through Radcliffe-Brown, who was a great admirer of them). I enjoyed Malinowski very much, loved him, but thought him a lousy anthropological theorist. Most of my colleagues (other than his students) hated his guts but were dreadfully afraid that he was a great theorist.

"In World War II, I came running back to England in September 1939 while Margaret was having a baby* in New York. I was promptly advised to return to America to help America join England. The Japanese finally did that for us. And I went through the war with the American Office of Strategic Services as a psychological planner. I don't think I helped the war much, but we did run four issues of an underground newspaper behind the Japanese lines in Burma.

"Oh yes, before I went overseas I had a job analyzing German propaganda films in the Museum of Modern Art, New York City, and just before going overseas, I had met Warren McCulloch and Bigelow, who were all excited about 'feedback'

* Mary Catherine Bateson

in electronic machinery. So while I was overseas, and mostly bored and frustrated, I occasionally comforted myself by thinking about the properties of closed self-corrective circuits. On arrival back in New York I went straight to the Macy Foundation to ask for a conference on these things. Fremont-Smith said, 'McCulloch was here a week ago with the same request, and he's going to be the chairman.' Membership in those conferences, with Norbert Wiener, John Von Neumann, McCulloch, and the rest, was one of the great events in my life. Wiener coined the word 'cybernetics' for what it was we were discussing.

"I was gently dropped from Harvard because a rumor got around, 'Bateson says anthropologists ought to be psychoanalyzed.' I did not say this, and I don't think I even believed it, but if they thought this was a good reason for dropping me, then I was probably lucky to be dropped. I was immediately picked up by Jurgen Ruesch for his research project in the Langley Porter Clinic, a psychiatric institution. This was the beginning of fourteen years of association with psychiatry, where I did my best, again, to bring formal theory into a very unformed Augean stable. The result was the so-called double bind hypothesis, which provided a framework for the formal description of schizophrenic symptoms and the experience of the schizophrenic in his family. I think this held up and still holds up pretty well in the face of a lot of misunderstanding and a little criticism. I am still pretty sure that something like the double bind story is an essential part of the phenomenon called 'schizophrenia.' In England my chief admirer in this field is Ronnie Laing. (By the way, you will probably run into rumors that Ronnie got too many of his ideas from me. I don't think this is really true. He certainly got some, and it is after all the purpose of scientific publication to spread ideas around, and I don't think he could at all be accused of plagiarism. I, too, have benefited by reading his stuff.)

"Enough mental hospitals and schizophrenic families is after a while enough, so I went off in 1963 to study dolphins, first

under John Lilly, and then in Hawaii with the Oceanic Institute. A fascinating but terribly difficult animal to study. But they forced me to straighten out my contributions to learning theory and what's wrong with B. F. Skinner. But alas, the Institute went broke.

"So here I am, corrupting the minds of the youth in the University of California at Santa Cruz. And also the minds of the faculty. I have a class for seventy students called 'The Ecology of Mind.' For this I have six section leaders, who are fully grown-up professors, a molecular biologist, an astronomer from Lick Observatory, a tidepool zoologist, a historian, a literary bloke, and a self-unfrocked Jesuit. What I mean is that my stuff is relevant and sometimes difficult for all sorts of people. On the whole, the students get more out of it than the grown-ups."

Fifty-odd pages of *The Evolutionary Idea* have arrived. It is April 1974. The material is dense and difficult. I have responded with faint praise and well-intentioned criticism, urging Bateson to open it up, be more chatty, try to include the human, the anecdotal, and so forth. I have asked if the format of a metalogue between a father and a young daughter is necessary. Why can't the ideas be presented in a more traditional form? Bateson's letter is biting:

"I have now your letter of April 16th, your long-distance telephone call of the day before yesterday, and some pieces of telephone talk in New York. All these tend in the direction of 'please be more prolix.' I tossed the first two chapters in the wastepaper basket at four o'clock this morning and shall probably do so again tomorrow. I think the real difficulty is that some readers (*et tu, Brute?*) just do not believe that I mean what I say. I suspect they think it is all a sort of entertainment and hope to come out at the end feeling refreshed. Believe me, John, that is not at all what it is about. Anybody who really reads and notices what is said and after several readings begins to understand it, will come out in despair and nearer to tears than laughter.

"In any case, my colleagues writing in the same field, whether terse or prolix, are incredibly difficult. The ideas which we deal with are difficult, painful, and foreign ideas. If you doubt this, I suggest a dose of Immanuel Kant as an example of the prolix, or a dose of Wittgenstein's *Tractatus* as an example of the terse. Honestly, I believe Kant is the more difficult.

"There are good and serious reasons why one party in the metalogues has to be in the period of sexual latency. This is not just in order to be cute; it is in order to be *acute*.

"For the rest, I will try not to let your remarks disturb me. I am, alas, too liable to let that sort of thing enrage me.

"There is a cute story going around about Picasso. A gent wanted him to paint things in a more representational manner, 'like this photograph of my wife. It is really like her.' Picasso looked at it and said, 'She is small, isn't she? And flat.' "

New technology equals new perception. The English biologist J. Z. Young points out that man creates tools and then molds himself in their image. Reality is manmade. An invention, a metaphor.

"The heart is a pump" is a statement we all accept as a truism. "The brain is a computer" is a statement that usually brings forth cries of humanistic horror. We seem to forget that the first statement is a creature of Newtonian mathematics. Newton created a mechanistic methodology. We invented ourselves in terms of its descriptive language. We don't say the heart is *like* a pump. The heart *is* a pump. The metaphor is operational.

Although many of us are not ready for it, within a few years we will all recognize that the brain *is* a computer. This will be a result of the cybernetic ideas developed by such men as Gregory Bateson, Norbert Wiener, Warren McCulloch, Gordon Pask, Ross Ashby, John Von Neumann, Heinz Von Foerster, and John Lilly, to name a few. New technology equals new perception. The words of the world are the life of the world. Nature is not created. Nature is said.

We are just now beginning to recognize the new order resulting from the development of the science of cybernetics. Bateson believes that the cybernetic explanation is the most important fundamental intellectual advance of the last two thousand years. It tears the fabric of our habitual thinking apart. Subject and object fuse. The individual self decreates. It is a world of pattern, of order, of resonances.

Bateson is special. He is the only living person fully equipped to construct a bridge between the world of nineteenth-century science and the cybernetic world of today. He has lived on both sides of the bridge. On one side, the solid world embodied by his father, William Bateson, on the other side, the undone world of Gregory Bateson, a world of language, communication, and pattern.

Bateson is sitting in my living room in May 1974. Today is his seventieth birthday. As we prepare for a big party, I suggest the possibility of organizing a book in his honor. "I hope that if there were such a book that it focus on the ideas and what they are doing to us," he says.

We talk and plan. Bateson gives his blessing to the project. *Steps to An Ecology of Mind* is by no means an easy or popular presentation of the core problems he has addressed himself to. We decide to invite a number of his friends and colleagues to contribute original essays, using *Steps* as a springboard, something either to disagree with or to take off from. Bateson writes a letter for the invitees. In the letter he suggests:

"Possible angles which the authors might cover include: changed perceptions of the Self; changed concepts of responsibility; changed feelings about time; money; authority; attitudes toward environment; sex; children; family; control and law; city planning; biological bases for human planning and ethics; the seeking of optimal and homeostatic goals rather than maxima; population control; changes in the balance between 'feelings' and 'intellect'; changes in educational methods; new horizons in psychiatry; etc., etc.

"The possible field is very wide, but in sum what I would like to see would be a thoughtful forum on the subject of what you all (and I, too) are doing to the premises of civilization."

Eight people, myself included, will contribute to the book. Mary Catherine Bateson (anthropologist and the daughter of Bateson and Margaret Mead), Ray L. Birdwhistell (expert in kinesics and communication), David Lipset (Bateson's authorized biographer), Rollo May (humanistic psychologist), Margaret Mead (anthropologist and Bateson's first wife), Edwin Schlossberg (physicist and environmental designer), and C. H. Waddington (geneticist). Unfortunately, Waddington dies before his piece is completed.

Other invited people are too busy with their own work or have problems with Bateson's ideas. His insistence on strict, as opposed to loose, thinking is most apparent with regard to his attitude toward his close friends and colleagues. It is December 1974, and I have just received his correspondence with a famous psychologist and author (who is not represented in this book). The psychologist plans to write about energy. "Everybody talks about it and nobody knows what it means," he says.

Bateson's response typifies the rigor of his precise thinking.

"You say 'energy' and qualify the word by saying that neither you nor anybody knows what it is.

"But that (the qualifying comment) is not quite true, because, after all, *we* (scientists) made up the concept and therefore know (or *should* know) what we put into it.

"What is on the other side of the fence, of course, we do not know. But we made the concept to cover what we thought was 'out there' and gave the concept what we thought were appropriate characteristics. These latter we *know,* because we put them where they are, inside that word 'energy.'

"I am strongly of the opinion that these well-known characteristics are not appropriate to the sort of explanatory principle which psychologists want to make of the concept.

"1) 'Energy' is a quantity. It is indeed rather like 'mass,' which is another quantity. Or 'velocity.' None of these is a 'substance' or a 'pattern.' They are quantities, *not* numbers.

"2) 'Energy' is a very tightly defined quantity, having the dimensions ML^2/T^2 (i.e., (mass × length × length) ÷ (time × time), or, more familiarly, mass × velocity^2).

"Now the rub is that no quantity can ever generate a pattern, and to assert that this can occur is precisely the entering wedge of the new supernaturalism, for which Freud, Marx, and Jung are much to blame. (They 'could' have known better.)

"Quantity, of course, can and often does develop and intensify latent difference but never creates that difference. Tension may find out the weakest link in the chain but it is never the explanation of how that particular link came to be the weakest. (Indeed the characteristic called 'being weakest' is not inherent in that link but precisely in the *relation* between that link and the others. 'It' could be 'protected' by filing one of the others!).

"3) The next step in supernaturalism after the invocation of 'energy' is the belief in Lamarckian inheritance and ESP. After that the next step is the assertion that man contains two real existing principles, viz., a Body and a Soul. After that, any sort of tyranny and oppression can be rationalized as 'good' for the victim."

"So there is a slot in our proposed book for arguments in favor of 'energy' as an explanatory principle, but such arguments in that context will necessarily be controversial. I urge you to treat 'energy' as a controversial issue, not as a 'matter-of-course.'

"Personally I have never been able to see or feel why this very 'mechanical' metaphor ('energy') appeals to especially humanistic psychologists. What are the arguments for this metaphor rather than 'entropy' (which is still a sort of quantity)? What characteristics of the original concept (energy or entropy) are to be carried over when the concept is used metaphorically to explain action or (?) anatomy?

"Are you familiar with Larry Kubie's paper,* long ago, in which he neatly and (I think) completely exploded the whole Freudian 'economics' of energy? It was that paper that earned him his place at the Macy Cybernetic conferences. But he never contributed anything there. I guess they slapped his wrist for heresy.

"Finally, believe me that the intensity of passion and care spent upon this letter is a function of both my esteem for you and my hatred of the principles which hide behind the use of 'energy' (and 'tension,' 'power,' 'force,' etc.) to *explain* behavior."

It is January 1977. The publisher has called. The book is overdue. The pieces have been written, discussed, and edited. They provide an excellent entry into areas of Bateson's thought. The contributors have measured his work in terms of its effect, in terms of information.

I call Bateson in Santa Cruz to discuss the introduction. Before we get down to business, he tells me that Governor Brown has just named him to the Board of Regents of the University of California. Also, Charles Roycroft, British psychoanalyst, is quoted in the Seventy-Fifth Anniversary Issue of the *Times Literary Supplement* as saying that Gregory Bateson is the most underrated writer of the past seventy-five years.

I would like to interview Bateson for the introduction, but this proves logistically impossible. Thus I must edit my thoughts, notes, and our correspondence to present him to the reader. The present piece, I realize, is hardly a comprehensive introduction to the man and his work. But, as Bateson might

* "Fallacious Use of Quantitative Concepts in Dynamic Psychology," *Psychoanalytic Quarterly* 16 (1947): 507–18.

say, it is a "step." It is important that readers realize that although this book is an introduction to Gregory Bateson, the only way to "get" Bateson is to read him. Study him. Editing this book has been, for me, most important. I found it necessary to force myself to sit quite still for many, many hours and study (not *read*) *Steps to an Ecology of Mind,* a rich, exhilarating experience. Roycroft is correct. Bateson is the most underrated writer of the century. To spend time with him, in person or through his essays, is rigorous intelligent exercise, an immense relief from the trivial forms that command respect in contemporary society.

I ask Bateson to write an afterword to the book. "What do you want me to write about?" he responds. I am most interested in his ideas on cybernetic explanation and epistemology. While pondering his question, I remember a conversation with cultural anthropologist Edward T. Hall, who pointed out to me that the most significant, the most critical inventions of man were not those ever considered to be inventions, but those that appeared to be innate and natural. To illustrate the point, he told a story of a group of cavemen living in prehistoric times. One day, while sitting around the fire, one of the men said, "Guess what? We're talking." Silence. The others looked at him with suspicion. "What's talking?" one of them asked. "It's what we're all doing. Right now. We're talking!" "You're crazy," another man replied. "Who ever heard of such a thing?" "I'm not crazy," the first man said, "you're crazy. We're talking." And it became a question of "who's crazy?" The group could not see or understand because "talking" was invented by the first man. The moment he said "We're talking" was a moment of great significance in the process of evolution.

A modern-day descendant of Hall's caveman is Gregory Bateson. He is busy inventing something, an invention so profound that once fully propounded, it will seem always to have been "natural." The full impact of Bateson's thinking is so radical that, yes, I have doubts that he fully believes in his own ideas. This is the way it has to be. He has entered no man's land. He is trying something new.

"We're talking."

Gregory Bateson: Early Biography

⚙ ⚙

DAVID LIPSET

David Lipset is the author of the forthcoming book tentatively called *A Tear Is an Intellectual Thing: A Biography of Gregory Bateson*. Mr. Lipset is a graduate student in anthropology at the University of California, San Diego. He lives in Del Mar, California.

"And when I passed by thee, and saw thee wallowing in thy blood, I said unto thee: In thy blood, live . . ."
(Ezekiel 16:6)

At the turn of the century, the edges of the Victorian intellectual world were beginning to curl. Rigid formalism was typically greeted by bohemian exhibition. Some of the literati were moving to Bloomsbury, partly the result of a scientific revolution two generations earlier, which often had replaced the Book of Genesis in men's minds with *The Origin of Species*. At Cambridge, the movement was reiterated in the contradictory quality of the community, which contained both generational continuity, intermarriage, as well as eclecticism and eccentricity. The circle of academic families that concerns us, the Darwins, Huxleys, Whiteheads, Haldanes, Hutchinsons, and, of course, the Batesons, all produced generation after generation of scholars, whose interests were wide ranging, and whose education had been intense. These were upper-middle-class professionals, well-to-do, self-satisfied, and devoted to the intellectual life. For the most part, their science was their religion and their offspring were expected to maintain their parents' faith.[1]

Gregory Bateson's grandfather, William Henry Bateson, (1812–1881) was ". . . the fifth son of Richard Bateson, a prosperous merchant of Liverpool. . . . [William Henry] was educated at Shrewsbury under Dr. Samuel Butler* and at St. John's College, Cambridge."[2] He became a vicar of the Anglican Church and was elected Master of St. John's in 1857.

> To be a master of a college, in those days you had to be a vicar. . . . He married a tiny, little girl, Anna Aikin,† she was one of the first suffragettes. Not only votes for women, but women's membership in the University and all of that. . . . She was a beauty. They had a . . . raft of preponderantly girls, most of them masculine, and two boys.[3]

One of the girls, Mary Bateson, became a prolific historian. Of the two boys, Edward Bateson became a judge and William (1861–1926), Gregory's father, was the leading English biologist and geneticist of his time.

As a youth, though, William's orchestration of his intellectual pursuit seemed not to have been appreciated by his father. In a letter to a friend, William Henry wrote the following about his sixteen-year-old son. The commentary is by the son's wife, Beatrice Bateson, fifty years later.

> I regard you as fortunate in one respect with regard to your son Robert, that he has a distinct and decided inclination for one pursuit in life. It is a great advantage where it exists and it can appropriately be gratified. We have been wishing that our eldest boy could manifest some special propension but as yet there are no signs of any . . . (1877)
>
> As a matter of fact, the boy knew very well what he wanted to try to do, but his experiences at school had not developed self-confidence. The remoteness of his interests from his father's doubtless contributed to the illusion of aimlessness.[4]

Years after William Henry's death, William Bateson described his father's character rather glowingly.

* The grandfather of the author of *The Way of All Flesh.*

† Of Anna's father, James Aikin, it has been said, ". . . there was no man who could so effectually silence an opposition by the vigour and readiness of his repartee . . ."[5]

> I wish you had known my father—he died while I was an undergraduate before even I knew how rare such men as he are in this world. He was the most unworldly of men, so thoughtful and gentle, and yet a strong clever man too. I know now that his ways must have been of the old regime, courtly and delicate—and yet he was essentially a man of action. Most of the changes made in Cambridge, bringing in the things of the new knowledge, have been more or less helped by him. A very few weeks before he died he sat day after day at the Arts School where the changes of the last Commission were being debated, and stood up and tackled the enemy on point after point, till at last no one could be got up against him. I have heard many men say that it was a regular rout; of course I knew nothing about these things then.[6]

When at university, William Bateson was said to have been enormously interested in ritual, "he was extraordinarily well-informed about the conduct and faith of the different sects. . . . He attended church and chapel and meeting house assiduously."[7] Psychical research also interested him deeply. "[William] watched, formed his conclusions, and stood aside; but he became an expert 'thought reader' and enjoyed 'performing.' "[8]

At maturity, Bateson had developed into what his wife later called "a rare personality."[9] He was an impersonal, aggressive, strongly and widely opinionated man. For example, in June 1886, he wrote to one of his sisters Anna (then studying botany),

> You are very thoughtful in thanking me for what little I have done, but in all seriousness, I often feel very heavy when I reflect that in all probability you would have done better, as regards class, if you had taken—History, "par example," but I console myself when I reflect that perhaps you would have despised such a success. And don't think that I mean to throw mud at Mary [a historian of some note] not at all—I am heartily glad she is doing so well and am proud of it too—but more because I don't think that she will make mere pot-boiling stuff

> of it, but also real work. But I believe that if you had been successful in such a subject, you would have regretted that your work did not lie a little nearer the origin of things, and was not, so to speak, "purer" than such work must be. And so I don't altogether regret for your sake, that I lead you in at such an infernally strait gate.[10]

Bateson was a sharp-tongued nonconformist. He deplored ordinary political activity, considering it futile, and a tool of the dull masses. His wife wrote that, as far as possible,

> he kept his attention steadily on his scientific work and avoided the motions which the public policy and events of the day stirred in him; indeed, for many years he ceased to read the newspaper regularly, buying one only when the housemaid demanded paper for her fire, or for amusement from matters such as a case in the Court of Arches, the doctrinal embarrassments of colonial Bishops, the Rougemont hoax, or the theft of a pearl.[11]

W.B., as his students called him, was completely unashamed about his intellectual elitism. "We have made the world safe for democracy," he wrote in 1918, "but have made it unsafe for anything else."[12] Specifically, he was concerned with the collapse of the European scientific community in the postwar period. The new standards were vulgar and utilitarian. It was a time when ". . . science was tolerated as a course of material advantage, when chaos [was] acclaimed as art, and learning [was] supplanted by schools of commerce."[13] Bateson regarded the major advances of Western civilization to be essentially the work of individual genius. He had no use for egalitarian trends. William Coleman, the historian of science, has written that "[he] spoke well of the intellectual elite."

> He was himself, of course, of that same class and doubtlessly high companionship in various ways colored his views. Bateson was, however, no shallow apologist. He sought always to portray aspiration, not present accomplishment. The realm of commonly unattainable vision and concomitant standards

> the genius might alone approach. It was his profound and his unflinching quest to attain them that marked him off from his fellows. . . . Bateson to a large degree was such an individual, yet he never assumed for himself, either directly or by implications, the role of genius. What was of paramount importance to him was the fact that the idea of genius allowed both definition and expression of his own deepest motivation.[14]

W.B. had excellent, if dogmatic, artistic taste. He deeply appreciated art. It was sacred to him. He "worshipped it, and regarded it as unaccessible to all but geniuses."[15] Bateson formed major collections of old master drawings, Japanese color prints, Greek Island embroideries, and lesser collections of Chinese porcelain and bronzes, and works by William Blake. "Of all pastimes," his wife wrote, "except that of painting, the hunting and acquisition of Old Master drawings was his favorite. He had an extraordinary sure 'flair' for a good thing, and once started, his collection grew and paid its own way."[16]

He knew the major European museums by heart, and though a highly successful scientist, he always tacitly felt envious of his literary and artistic friends, whose traditions he had not the time to possess. Again Coleman,

> Master drawings, Oriental prints, and objects d'art and the graphics and work of William Blake shared [the] paramount quality of total exposure, were we sufficiently acute to see it, of the artists' intentions. In these objects, supreme of their kind, the individual creative genius shared with mankind distinctive and instinctive recognition of the way things truly are or should be. [*For Bateson*] *intuitive genius culminated in artistic genius.*[17] [italics mine]

At the age of thirty-five, William Bateson married Beatrice Durham. In retrospect, she wrote, "in June 1896, we were married, and I began to learn what life may be."[18] Her father was an alcoholic and her mother, a "puritan." "[There was] a long line of six or seven sisters of which Beatrice was among the first. Dick was the eldest. She was quite masculine. Papa was a distinguished surgeon, chief surgeon of Guys Hospital in London. And the children were given to believe that the coachman was an alcoholic. The coachman and the surgeon would come in arm in arm in the middle of the night. But in fact it was the coachman supporting the surgeon and not vice versa."[19] If William was virulent and extroverted, Beatrice was shy and reserved. They had three sons—John (1898–1918),* Martin (1900–1922), and Gregory, who was born on May 4, 1904, in Grantchester, England.

"I grew up in the middle of Natural History, and beetle collecting and all of that. This was the culture of the house. There was no question."[21] The Bateson family was steeped in the biological sciences and William Bateson was the director of research. His wife wrote, "his standard of accuracy was rigid and high,"

> and he exacted critical carefulness from his helpers, both students and garden staff, in all their operations and experiments. He himself with fine, sensitive hands was a beautiful manipulator. To watch him at work, delicately dissecting some fragile blossom, was a splendid lesson. *He seldom bungled.*[22] [italics mine]

William's science was a very personal one. He did not maintain a division between his work and his "private life." Childhood in his household was an informal but full-time course in the father's natural science. The children were trained to be naturalists, it would seem, in lieu of being allowed to be children. Walks were considered to be field trips, and conversations were explicitly didactic. In somewhat typical Victorian fashion, the Bateson family was exceedingly constrained and ordered. William was a widely dogmatic man and his family was organized around his orthodoxies, however contradictory and paradoxical.

Gregory was born during the beginning of his father's in-

* "In 1898," Beatrice wrote, "our first child was born, an event commemorated by the purchase of Blake's *Book of Job*."[20]

volvement with the rediscovery of Mendel's genetics.* "William Bateson of Cambridge read about Mendel's paper coming up to London, in the train, on April 8, 1900. He saw at once, if not all the implications, at least a great part of it."[23] W.B.'s commitment to the Mendelian case was exceptionally strong. He believed that Gregor Mendel's peas held the validation of the science of heredity, and named his youngest son Gregory, in honor of the hero.

Gregory, then, was born into the stable, formal world of Cambridge intellectuals dominated by three elements: 1) the scientific exuberance and social prominence of his father, 2) his two elder brothers, John and Martin, and 3) William Bateson's relationship to the nineteenth-century traditions of the biological sciences.

He was fascinated by and afraid of his father, and said to have been "like a third to twins" to his two elder brothers. "It was they," Margaret Mead has said, "who received all the attention, and it was they who were considered to be the clever ones."[24]

> I was always the stupid one. Or believed myself to be labeled so. I think I probably was. . . . He [W.B.] was always a little embarrassed [by me]. . . . I had the results of my [college] examination sent home. I had gotten a first on my Tripos [honors examination]. He hemmed and hawed and said "It's nice to know you are a little better than the others, Gregory."[25]

As children, the two elder brothers spent much time on field trips, observing wildlife, during which they taught Gregory what they had begun to learn about the natural sciences.

They were completely dependent on their nanny and were taught to pay strict respect to their father, in part by silent attention to his monologic performances during meals. "Working as he did almost entirely at home," their mother wrote,

* Mendel first described, in 1865, the formal mechanics of heredity, but was completely ignored by the scientific community for thirty-five years.

> the children saw much of their father, and he very soon established a delightful camaraderie with them. He was keenly interested in watching their development, and enjoyed helping them. *He was determined that their education should be based on literature.* Every morning for many years he read them after breakfast, generally from the Old Testament, but sometimes from Bunyan or other fine prose, or even from Shakespeare. If sometimes he rose from the table, absent-minded, one of them would say, "We haven't had our chapter, father," and back he came.[26] [italics mine]

Gregory, on the other hand, recalled that it was not so warm an atmosphere to have grown up in. "It was really embattled, a lot of squawking."[27] The family valued intellect, but did not associate it with physical intimacy. The one time Gregory remembers touching his father was wiping his nose after he died.

They were self-assured people, imbued, to a certain extent, with a sense of intellectual destiny. For example W.B. wrote the following letter to his eldest son, John, on the occasion of his entry into boarding school (1907).

> Dear John,
>
> I have just got letters from your mother, from which I hear that by now you must be a real schoolboy! That is a great state in life and I hope that you have made a good beginning and are working hard. *The great thing is to go your own way and not to bother what other people think or say about you. If you are satisfied that what you do is right, you can't go very far wrong.*
>
> I am afraid butterflies are quite over—at least for the present. I saw a "tufted grouse" in the woods. It was close to me, such a fine big bird. I have seen three kinds of squirrels in U.S.A. . . .[28] [italics mine]

From the parents there was "no expectation that we would be any good but there was a strong feeling that we ought to be."[29]

They were a completely godless family, except, perhaps, in

their devotion to science. Beatrice, Gregory's mother, was a fourth-generation atheist. And though W.B.'s father had been a vicar, he has been described more as a university politician than as a man of God. In any case, William Bateson was a confirmed atheist throughout Gregory's time en famille. "W.B. knew something about the sort of structure of the Anglican creed, *about the nature of heresy and things of this kind.* . . . The old man used to read us the Bible at breakfast, because he maintained that we should not grow up to be empty-headed atheists."[30] (italics mine)

In 1910, the Batesons moved to Merton outside London, where the John Innes Horticultural Institute was located. After two years in the new neighborhood, Gregory began to pick up the local accent, which irritated his father (accent, in England, being a class distinction). It was decided to send him to Wardenhouse, which was a quite religious boarding school (as were they all at that time). Gregory remembered:

> My mother saw that there was a crisis ahead. There was very little use to ask my father about it. So she handed me over to my brothers for religious education. They took me for a walk . . . and told me that at school I would probably sleep in a dormitory, and that I'd better watch what the other boys did, that when they knelt down to pray that I should do the same. And that if I said the alphabet over eight times, that that would be long enough and then I could get up. *So I went to school with complete authoritarian approval, for conforming to that which I did not believe in.*[31] [italics mine]

At the age of fourteen, in 1918, Gregory went on to board at Charterhouse. His eldest brother, John, meanwhile, had joined the army. He was killed at the end of World War I, in Flanders (October, 1918). Beatrice Bateson described him in a brief epitaph: "John, field naturalist, of uncommonly ripe judgment and good promise of scientific ability."[32] And W.B. wrote to Martin,

> I know what you must be feeling. John was a splendid creature; such breadth and balance are rare in men so young. He

> would have been a comrade for life to you and his mother. Like all of us I think he had no illusions [about the war]. I never heard him say a foolish thing even when quite little, and he knew how to bear trouble. . . . There never was a nobler soul.[33]

Martin, who was eighteen at the time of his brother's death, had been a conscientious objector. The course of events is unclear, but we find him in the military at the end of the war. Gregory is unsure but supposes that William "pushed" him in. When John died, Martin had raged at his father,[34] to which William had replied:

> A skipper has to put his ship's safety first, and during the critical moments the only chance in the long run is for the objector to subordinate his opinion and do what he is ordered to do. Sophistry and casuistical reasoning may be used in representing occasions as critical which are not critical, and vice versa, but in 1914 the moment, as I have said, was in my judgment most certainly critical in every sense of the word. . . . The spirit in which we have carried on the war is enough to make anyone sick and ashamed of their country. But that I believe is the line we have usually taken in recent wars. It certainly was so in the Boer war, and I believe in the Crimea also.
>
> *It is always a prominent thought in my mind that strictly speaking such people as we are do not belong and are only here on sufferance.* To think for oneself in most societies is a crime. But there it is! One has just to make the best of the situation and be thankful we are allowed our niche.[35] [italics mine]

Martin returned from the war still extremely disillusioned by his brother's death and by what he called, "the bullying of the inheritance"[36]—by his feeling that, despite his overriding interest in the theater, he would succumb to the weight of his father's search for a successor. In fact, he went up to Cambridge and passed his Tripos in Biology with a brilliant first. But Martin's concerns were not scientific: He wanted to be a playwright. This preoccupation precipitated a bitter fight with his father. The following is Gregory's account:

> W.B.'s view of literature and the arts was that they were the great thing in the world but that no Bateson would ever be capable of contributing to them. Art, to him, meant the Renaissance, pretty nearly, and of course nobody in the twentieth century could make Renaissance art. But science was something which one could do. *It was more conscious.* It didn't depend on genius, genius being some sort of demon inside you. So Martin quarreled with W.B. about going to drama school. . . . [nonetheless] he went. There he fell in love with a lady who was already engaged. And he made a tremendously dramatic fuss about it, in which he finally made a date with himself . . . that he would go to see her on John's birthday, as a final attempt to persuade her, and if she would not have him he would shoot himself. In fact, she wouldn't, and he went out into the middle of Piccadilly Circus, put a revolver to his head, and shot himself, *under a statue of Eros.*[37] [italics mine]

Beatrice described her husband's response to his son's suicide:

> In April of that year [1922] we lost our second boy. Months of despondency and dejection followed. Even the garden and laboratories almost failed to rouse him. But, happily, a new interest began at this time to push into his life.
>
> In May 1922 he was unanimously elected to be a Trustee of the British Museum. This honour gave him extraordinary pleasure; it was an expression of confidence that he felt he must stir himself to justify. No foreign travel or medical regime could have helped him as did this unexpected appointment. Gradually, from fortnight to fortnight, his interest in his new responsibility grew, and with his interest grew his pleasure.
>
> From boyhood he had been a devotee of Museums . . . whether of Natural History, objects of art, or pictures. . . . Perhaps no distinction in the world would have gratified him more. His energy and his spirit grew again. *The honour of*

> *Knighthood also was offered to him in May 1922, but this he declined.*[38] [italics mine]

Gregory had thus become sole heir to an ambiguous intellectual heritage in the natural sciences. Personified to him by his father, this tradition resembled nineteenth-century biology in its wide-ranging qualitative ideas connected with the theory of evolution and the variation of species. Its devotees included not only cautious, thorough, empirical scientists, such as Charles Darwin, but also more literary intellectuals actively concerned with science, such as Samuel Butler, as well as men like Lamarck who were both qualitative and empirical.[39] Coleman has written:

> Reflecting upon the thought and practice of English . . . [science] . . . towards century's end, the French physicist and historian, Pierre Duhem, detected there an ampleness which the more "geometrical" disposition of the Continental savants appeared to lack. The Englishman understood nature not in terms of abstract relations but through direct representation of events. He must "see" to understand. The use of the physical model is introduced. Kelvin's opinion that understanding an event really means, "Can we form a model of that event?" elicited Duhem's notable characterization of the English view as the "victory of imagination over reason."[40]

Particular to William Bateson was a vigilantly individualistic commitment to natural science that seemingly had its inspiration in intuition and personal style, but which fervently denied this foundation. He had "something of that burning passion for truth, of that high conception of the calling of the naturalist. . . . [This] was the essence of Bateson's personality."[41]

> [As a scientist William] was essentially *a man of intuitions and convictions*. The intuition of some scientific men runs sympathetically with the working of the natural universe, and they contribute to knowledge leading ideas which experi-

> ments hasten to verify. Others only arrive by plodding strenuous analysis of phenomena until the unity within them is laid bare, free of the diversities which obscured it. Bateson was one of the former gifted type, and his enthusiasms were for clearcut new ideas. . . . He was impatient of expositions which involved elaborate quantitative treatments and then still leave residual suspense accounts. . . . *Never one for half measures or compromises,* it sometimes happened that when he was up against men of older generations whose views were inflexible, he could make no progress, but only camp out against them in stubborn opposition. This is a situation which makes for little personal happiness in a scientific community, and Bateson certainly sacrificed something for his faiths.[42] [italics mine]

Like many English scholars before and since, William Bateson was emotionally involved with the intellect and was intellectually (i.e., detachedly) involved with emotion. It is too strong to say that he was a cold man with other people, for he was loved by many. But to say that his emotions were largely reserved for his science and, except in crisis, not articulately expressed in interpersonal contexts, is a more accurate description of the man. For example, having broken through some vexing problem, he wrote Beatrice, "I feel rather like I did on the morning of January 11, 1889 [the day of their engagement]—very pleased with myself—only perhaps a little more certain I am on the right track. Also the risks incurred are not so great, because hypothesis can be amended—wives less easily."[43] Conversely, he was reticent to permit the entry of what he called "the vicissitudes of human life" into his scientific endeavor. Like Yeats, who turned to mystical reverie as a defensive shell against his father's belligerent rationalism,* William Bateson used his science as protection against an abusive universe. He wrote:

* Yeats wrote, "Arguments with my father, whose convictions had been formed by John Stuart Mill's attack upon Sir William Hamilton, had destroyed my confidence and driven me from speculation to the direct experience of the mystics."[44]

> We are all men born into a splendid and terrible world in which for a while our lot is to enjoy and to suffer. The one reasonable aim of man is that life shall be as happy as it can be made, with as much as possible of job and as little as possible of pain. *There is only one way of attaining that aim; the pursuit of natural knowledge.*[45] [italics mine]

"One could not imagine, whilst working with him," his wife said, "that he had any trouble or anxiety greater than the sterility of a pea, or the death of a valued chick. In the garden and the poultry pen, vexation, worry, and annoyance were all forgotten; he could not be ruffled by outside . . . disturbance."[46]

William saw science as an explorer might anticipate a voyage; with a combination of apprehension, contention, elation, and resolution.

> Research was one long delicious adventure to him. He was patient, painstaking and ingenious—the drudgery was nought compared to the exhilarating thrill of treasure-trove, which sure enough awaited him. And yet as he worked, in the *white heat of excitement,* judgment sat within him cool and critical. *Emotion could not compel him to unwary haste.* Something of this pleasure of achievement though perhaps in less degree and without the magnificence of exaltation, moved him at auction sales, when *"backing his judgment against the room" he snatched a bargain from under the dealers' noses.*[47] [italics mine]

The analogy between William's emotional response to scientific discovery and his emotional response to obtaining a bargain at an auction is both intriguing and enlightening, and, as we shall see, shall serve as an apt guide to the epistemological and methodological side of his science. Initially, the auction context is one in which bidder tries to gratify his taste of pocketbook. It is a nonreflective situation, within the context. The bidder knows the depth of his means but he does not question the content of his taste. Ideally, the auction is impersonal, competitive, and isolating. It is a democratic free market, in which the buyer's knowledge is the sole determinant of an object's value. And to those who are self-righteously aware of the obscure, treasure is available.

As if on the edge of his seat, ready to bid on a little-known drawing, William wrote:

> If I may throw out a word of counsel to beginners, it is: *Treasure your exceptions!* When there are none, the work gets so dull that no one cares to carry it further. Keep them always uncovered and in sights. Exceptions are like the rough brickwork of a growing building which tells that there is more to come and shews [*sic*] where the next construction is to be.[48] [italics mine]

In the last decades of the nineteenth century, when William Bateson began his career in biology, the Darwinian corpus was undergoing a serious crisis. Retrospectively, Bateson described the situation, "In the study of evolution, progress had well-nigh stopped. The more vigorous, perhaps the more prudent, had left this field of science to labour in others, where the harvest is less precarious or the yield more immediate. Of those who remained some still struggled to push forward the truth through the jungle of phenomena: most were content supinely to rest on the great clearing Darwin made long since."[49]

Nevertheless, with characteristic single-mindedness, Bateson set out to explore the Russian Steppe (Lake Balkhash, Lake Tschalka, Aral Sea, and so on) in an effort to test what resembled a Lamarckian hypothesis to which he subscribed. Bateson's first scientific venture was inconclusive. Gregory Bateson told Arthur Koestler the following:

> As to whether my father was a nice man, in spite of natural ambivalence, I incline to say yes. He certainly was liked by many people who were undoubtedly nice people. But notably those who liked him were in general not his colleagues. Many of the latter hated his guts.
>
> He was certainly not a nice man whenever the inheritance

> of acquired characteristics was mentioned. When this happened the coffee cups rattled on the table. Remember that he went to the [Siberian] Steppe in order to prove the inheritance of acquired characteristics, using as data the creatures which he was going to find in Lake Balkhash, etc. The project was a complete failure. Perhaps this had something to do with his later attitude. I think he always knew that there was something very wrong with orthodox Darwinian theory, but at the same time he regarded Lamarckism as a tabooed pot of jam to which he was not allowed to reach. I have his copy of *The Origin of Species,* sixth edition, in which he listed on the fly-sheet the pages on which Darwin slipped into Lamarckian heresy.[50]

William thus rephrased his quest. "To solve the problem of the forms of living things," he wrote, "is the aim with which the naturalist of today [1893] comes to his work. How have living things become what they are, and what are the laws which govern their form?"[51]

> Behind Bateson's general views lies a marked visual bias. He was before all else a morphologist; here it was that he found his first problems and defined his scientific standards. "The geneticist," emphasized Bateson, "is the successor of the morphologist." Animal and plant form and their production become matters of highest prize. Biology, he insisted, must ever return to its "rightful place," that is, "investigation of the structure and properties of the concrete visible world."[52]

Coleman rightly divides W.B.'s career into three periods. The first, when he was concerned with morphology, shows Bateson as *enfant terrible.* "Formed by a rigid evolutionary orthodoxy, he came to deny . . . its objective and then its methods. His conclusions were unwelcome, and his outspoken manner, conveying harsh and ironic assaults upon Britain's pride, Darwinism as it triumphed in its second generation, further reduced the young man's appeal to more straightforward zoologists. This was Bateson the radical . . ."[53] By 1897, he had begun to experiment with plant hybridization.

This work "fitted in . . . with extraordinary nicety"[54] with the newly rediscovered work of Gregor Mendel. Bateson entered his Mendelian decade (1900–1910), pioneering the subject in England. He read Mendel's paper "Experiments in Plant Hybridization" while en route to deliver a lecture to the Royal Horticultural Society. He quickly rewrote his remarks in light of the new findings. Bateson's response to Mendel's peas is illustrated in the preface of his book *Mendel's Principles of Heredity: A Defense.*

> . . . two years ago it was suddenly discovered that an unknown man, Johann Gregor Mendel [sic], had, *alone and unheeded, broken off from the rest.* This is no metaphor, it is a simple fact. Each of us now looks at his own patch of work and sees Mendel's clue running through it; whither the clue will lead we dare not yet surmise.[55] [italics mine]

During this second period, Bateson finally won support for the course of his work. By 1908 he held a readership in zoology and then he accepted a term professorship in genetics, the first such chair in Britain. "In 1910 Bateson was offered, and accepted the directorship of the recently founded John Innes Horticultural Institution. The Institute offered better research opportunities than the University had or could and Bateson, while attached to Cambridge town, *was notably less so to the University.*"[56] (italics mine)

> *Always impatient himself of any arbitrary restraint,* he set none upon his staff, assuming from the first that only those students who wanted to work would come. All the facilities for which he had longed in past years were placed without stint before them; his confidence in them and his interest in their work were sufficient to make rules and regulations superfluous. There were none.[57] [italics mine]

The third period of Bateson's career was one in which he stressed non-Mendelian phenomena. He took up vigorous defensive action against the rising chromosome theory, and elaborated many of the positions of his pre-Mendelian inquiries. Controversy, as always, surrounded him. The Americans withdrew at his patent anti-Darwinism, and others "publicly regretted his to them obtuse criticism of the chromosome theory."[58]

> [During this period] . . . a dread of continued ignoble jealousies and hate made him appear unduly pessimistic to many of his friends; probably the suspicion that he, for one, could not live long enough to see goodwill restored between the nations added to his unhappiness. *But he never let his vexed and grieving spirit break the continuity of his scientific work; that went steadily on.* His despondency shewed [*sic*] itself in a demeanor more grave and serious, his lessened bodily health somewhat undermined his confidence, but his interest and enthusiasm never flagged.[59] [italics mine]

Thus we have seen that the analogy of the auction-goer, backing his knowledge and judgment against the house, provides a reasonable illustration of W.B.'s relationship to his scientific contemporaries. Here was the individualist among the impersonal; a man whose admiration of the work of other isolates (e.g., Blake and Mendel) was no less reiterated in his own behavior. Moreover, as would the bidder, Bateson's science was a continuous struggle to gratify his aesthetic taste. "If there had been no poets," he wrote in 1891,

> there would have been no problems, for surely the unlettered scientist of today would never have found them. To him it is easier to solve a difficulty than to feel it.[60]

For Bateson, *the seer,* in the nonconformist, the prophetic, the poetic, and the visual sense, had his place in science.

> To see meant to grasp spatial relations; form and not empty number or discordant matter was all important. *Formal relations were the province of aesthetic sensibility and hence art writ large would naturally and rightly assume a prescriptive role, in all our truly rational activity.* Reason was to be no

> mere matter of shuffling concrete sense impressions; it was the intuitive grasp of essential relations. Explanation, therefore, could only be "satisfying," that was its limit, but it was the highest possible limit. Experimental verification was appropriate for facts, even possibly minor hypotheses. On a more significant level, however, that at which the sensitive mind must operate, dogmatic canons of empirical verifiability or falsifiability failed because [they were] irrelevant.[61] [italics mine]

Perhaps the most personally damaging controversy Bateson engaged in, was his battle on the one hand to describe a formal "hereditary mechanism," and on the other to counter those who saw the basis of heredity in the concrete, i.e., in chromosomes. In this struggle, which spanned the last twenty-five years of William Bateson's life, we may observe his deeply felt aesthetic combine with his strength of character.

Throughout his career, William had maintained a strong anti-utilitarian, anti-Benthamite bias. "An exalted reverence for truth and beauty inspired him throughout his work," Beatrice wrote: "for Newton and Pasteur he had deep veneration, and for other giants of the annals of science too, but on the whole he rated scientific attainment lower in the scale of human achievement than that of the great Masters of art."[62] Of the Old Master drawings at Dresden, Bateson wrote:

> When you see them, you see well enough why lots of things in pictures don't come up to scratch, simply because they were done for the world, while the man did the drawings for himself. *All the drivel and half-heartedness of the pictures is away from the drawings. The fellows that did them, did them for outright love of them, and because they couldn't help it, and not for money and fame, as they did their pictures.*[63] [italics mine]

The drawing was expressive of basic meaning, whereas the painting was deceptive, brash, and worst of all, was done for *money*. Here was William's antimaterialism given an aesthetic meaning; it appeared no less zealously in his science, as we shall see.

> Materialism, while less conspicuous in Britain than on the Continent, accorded well with easy utilitarian values. It drew, moreover, welcome support from rampant nineteenth-century scientism. To many it appeared that science, whatever be its particular accomplishments, had found the way to truth. It was, in exaggeration, hard facts versus values. The popular mind and its representatives within the scientific profession were not, however, without critics. Academic philosophy turned in the 1870's to idealism. Hegel came to England. Others within and without the intellectual classes reacted principally to the social ramifications of the prevalent moral doctrine. Bateson, philosophically unsophisticated, but quite certain where the true merits of man and society must lie, relentlessly attacked the utilitarian spectre. In the quality of mind sympathetic to this social philosophy originated Bateson's complex aestheticism. . . . It no less encouraged his anti-materialistic stance and quest for a non-particulate, hence, given contemporary definitions, non-material basis of inheritance.[64]

Most bluntly, Bateson refused to admit the possibility of a material basis for heredity and variation. "In Nature," he wrote, "the body of one individual has never *been* the body of its parent." Rather "the new body is made again new from the beginning just as if the wax model had gone back to the melting pot before the new model was begun."[65] In constant opposition to all chromosome theory, and to all biological explanation that admitted Newtonian matter, Bateson stressed pattern and form, *the modus operandi* of which was to be motion and force or in his language, "vibrations."

> More personal and doubtlessly more influential contact with tendencies in physical thought at Cambridge came through long and intimate friendship with his Grantchester neighbor, Alfred North Whitehead. They shared not only interest and understanding of art and the classics but concern for a pressing problem: how to reconcile pattern or form, the product or companion of changes in geometry, with the inescapable dynamism of nature. From the rhythmic model Bateson aspired

to derive biological form from physical process; Whitehead's interest in the matter implicates his entire metaphysics.[66]

Bateson *tacitly* defined the problem of the mechanics of heredity and variation holistically. The organism was seen as an integral whole, not as an atomic assemblage of "characters." Moreover, the accurate reproduction of pattern was taken as a definition of heredity and alteration of the expected regularities stood for variation. Thus seen, the problem was laid open to solution in physical terms, by the use of the *visual analogies.* "We commonly think," Bateson wrote in 1907,

> of animals and plants as matter, but they are really systems through which matter is continually passing. *The orderly relations of their parts are as much under geometric control as the concentric waves spreading from a splash in a pool.* If we could in any real way identify or analyze the causation of growth, biology would become a branch of physics.[67] [italics mine]

At both the grosser phenotypic and the cellular levels, Bateson stressed the phenomena of division. "The greatest advance that we can foresee" he wrote,

> will be made when it is found possible to connect the geometrical phenomena of development with the chemical. The geometrical symmetry of living things is the key to a knowledge of their regularity, and the forces which cause it. In the symmetry of the dividing cell the basis of that resemblance we call Heredity is contained. *To imitate the morphological phenomena of life we have to devise a system which can divide.* It must be able to divide, and to segment as—grossly—a vibrating plate or rod does, or as an icicle can do as it becomes ribbed in a continuous stream of water; but with this distinction, that the distribution of chemical differences and properties must simultaneously be decided and disposed in orderly relation to the pattern of the segmentation.[68] [italics mine]

In sum, Bateson repeatedly argued that the hereditary mechanism was analogous to the systematic process by which symmetrical repetition of parts was produced, and conversely, that variation was comparable to differentiation between parts. Force within geometric form seems to have been the core of all Bateson's analogies. The source of the force or "rhythms of division," and therefore the source of heritable qualities was "polarity." Polarity as it was generally understood by nineteenth-century biologists,

> was the "force" generated between two poles of opposite sign or a dialectic established within a unitary focus of force. These poles might be real or, as was more commonly the case, ideal. To the steady and unidirectional exertion of this force was due the production of all natural phenomena. *Disturbances in the field of force gave rise to corrective tendencies. Although new positions of equilibrium would, barring new intrusive forces, ultimately be established, the road towards stability was marked by regular oscillations.* This conception was first given full articulation by the German Naturphilosophen early in the century.[69] [italics mine]

Bateson's use of a vibratory theory of heredity brought him into a tradition that had been continually on the verge of introducing psychic elements. In fact, one of his heroes, Samuel Butler, heartily supported the analogy between heredity and memory. Bateson, though, refused to accept any species of psyco-physical postulate. He wrote, "It is tempting to suppose that the apparatus, the readiness to make the right response to various stimuli, is a manifestation of unconscious memory, but since . . . there is no good reason to suppose that even the simplest experiences of the parent are . . . transmitted to a succeeding generation, the suggestion of continuous memory . . . can only be defended on grounds which to the biologist are mystical and unconvincing."[70]

He was a master of leaving the greatest things unsaid. "If you want to put salt on a bird's tail," said Gregory Bateson,

> "you will be well advised not to look at the bird while you approach it." His father, he continued, was "always trying to put salt on the tail of nature and particularly to catch that component of nature which we might as well call Mind." Bateson, however, did not discuss Mind. He skirted the issue, while always keeping an eye cocked upon it.[71] [italics mine]

Accordingly, Gregory Bateson writes that from conversation with his father, "and especially from the overtones of his talk,"[72] he garnered the tools and principles of scientific thinking. Thus, the son wrote,

> [W.B.] himself was inarticulate about philosophy and mathematics and logic, and he was articulately distrustful of such subjects, but still, in spite of himself, I think he passed on to me something of these matters. . . . *The attitudes I got from him were especially those which he denied in himself.* In his early—and as I think he knew—his best work he posed the problems of animal segmentation, serial repetition of parts, patterns, etc. Later he turned from this field into Mendelism, to which he devoted the remainder of his life. *But he always had a hankering after the problems of pattern and the mysticism that inspired it that I picked up* and which, for better or worse, I call science.[73] [italics mine]

Starting from an unarticulated holistic premise, William had tried to reconcile static form and pattern with the inescapable dynamism of nature. Visual analogies were his control tool, and phenomena that evidenced rhythmic order (the striped zebra, sand ripples on the beach, waves, and so on) suggested that heredity and variation might be formally comparable. Through the use of analogy one might also avoid precise definition of the sort of relations sought. Though he occasionally mistook his analogies for actual explanation, W.B. saw that ultimately, he was unable to solve his problem. As he mystified the intuitionist source of his own creativity, so evolutionary creativity was incomprehensible to him. "He was really unconscious of the unconscious processes of science."[74] Nevertheless, Bateson wrote in 1922, "Let us proclaim in unmistakable language that our faith in evolution is unshaken."

> Every line of argument converges on the inevitable conclusion; the obscurantist has nothing to suggest which is worth a moment's attention. The difficulties which weigh upon the professional biologist need not trouble the layman. Our doubts are not as to the reality of the truth of evolution, but as to the origin of *species* [italics his], a technical almost domestic problem. Any day that mystery may be solved. The discoveries of the last twenty-five years enable us for the first time to discuss these questions intelligently and on a basis of fact. *Synthesis will follow analysis. We do not and cannot doubt.*[75] [italics mine]

Gregory entered St. John's College at Cambridge in 1922, where the dominant intellectual trend in the biological sciences was to the eclectic. His classmates G. B. Hutchinson, C. H. Waddington, and Joseph Needham (slightly his senior) have all, like Gregory, retained wide-ranging scholarly interests. Bateson graduated in 1924, taking his examinations in zoology. He then left for the Galapagos Islands, and was baffled by the experience. He found there that he did not know what to do with field natural history. "I went to Galapagos and came back feeling very restive about sitting in a lab for the rest of my life."[76] At this time, W.B. pressured him to continue in the natural sciences. Something of this sentiment is reflected in the elder Bateson's response to a note, urging him, despite his age (sixty-five), to continue as director of the John Innes Institute (January 8, 1926).

> When I came here first I looked forward to doing much more than had been accomplished. Nor can I lay the blame for deficiencies wholly on the bad times through which we have passed. When the centre [*sic*] of chief interest in Genetics shifted away from work of my own type, to that of the American group, I was already *too old and too much fixed* in my ideas to become master of so very new and intricate a development. It has taken me years even to assimilate the new

> things and I recognize that the Institution has a right to a younger man in my place.
>
> But another shortcoming which may be even more serious is that I have not myself succeeded in bringing forward such a man, one I mean who might carry on the Institution somewhat on the lines we have hitherto followed. This anxiety has been continually in my thoughts and doubtless also in yours. The causes of the failure I need not now discuss. There are fashions in all things especially research, and just now those who in our day would have been zoologists or botanists are bio-chemists, almost every one. Having been so long disappointed I am not sanguine that in the short time that remains I can succeed, but I shall make the question of a successor more and more my first preoccupation.[77] [italics mine]

In 1925 W.B. and Gregory collaborated on a paper dealing with the pattern and symmetry of colors in the feathers of red-legged partridges.[78] For William, this was a return to his initial area of interest, and it was part of an admission that he had pursued Mendelian genetics mistakenly. "He confessed about a year before he died, that what is now called morphogenesis was the only thing he'd ever done that was any good, that this was where his work mattered. [It was] a feeling that he had followed a wrong lead."[79]

Gregory had been left, by his brothers' deaths and by his father's insistence, feeling crushed by the responsibility of his background.

> [I felt] I was getting breaks undeservedly. This was one of the reasons I moved out of zoology. . . . To get out of that field . . . to get into something in which I was me and not son of. . . . It bothered me a great deal, at the time. It used to bother me that I was named Gregory, after Gregor Mendel.[80]

He began to grope about, in an attempt to involve himself in something concerning people. "I tried psychology and that didn't make much sense. And I joined the Cambridge antiquarian society."[81] One of the early British field anthropologists, A. C. Haddon, jokingly offered him a year's training in social anthropology. Bateson took the offer seriously and accepted. By 1926 he had received the automatic M.A. in anthropology, which was, at the time, an inchoate quasi science concerned with experiential rather than genetic explanations of behavior. In an effort to discover what his son was doing, W.B. read Malinowski's *Argonauts of the Western Pacific* until he came upon an incident in which the Trobrianders burned an opossum alive. "He was absolutely disgusted . . . refusing to look any further. . . . He disapproved totally."[82]

> The switch to anthropology was sort of a revolt as far as I was concerned. And in a sense I didn't revolt very far, but it seemed further. [I did not want] to make a frontal attack, because I don't think the parents had any idea . . . what they were doing [to me]. . . . *But instead [I wanted] to use the sorts of tools that they would use to prove a new position. . . . That's the middle line I have been taking.*[83] [italics mine]

During his graduate work, Bateson became obsessed with William Blake. Though his father had owned and prominently displayed an original Blake painting ("Satan Exulting Over Eve") over the mantelpiece in their living room, Gregory thought of this study as the first of his own. As his father had rediscovered Mendel, Gregory believed in a way that he had rediscovered Blake. "He somehow felt that, instead of having his hands picked up and put on the keys of the piano, that with Blake he was free to pick it himself."[84] It is important to note that, in part, Blake developed his own very individualistic and obscure mythology, which was largely unaccepted by his contemporaries, who considered him mad.

William Bateson died in February 1926. In the following year, the anthropologist Haddon sent Gregory to do field work in New Guinea. "In fact, I fled from my mother. The two of them together [his parents] kind of neutralized each other somewhat. But after [W.B.] died, she took on the worst of his mannerisms with the rigidity of a convert. [My mother] had the whole thing rigged in which I was to become the precise reincarnation of the old man."[85] For Gregory, the conclusion of his upbringing may have been the realization that he was unsuited for Batesonian life. "I was born," he has said,

> with all the entree into the Bloomsbury group: Darwin, Virginia Woolf, etc., which was the network, really, that ran British science and intellectual life. But I never could bear to be *more than one foot into it*. I enjoyed playing the parlor games. But I ran away from it. . . . There's a dream which I had in the early thirties somewhere. In which *Freeman*, which was Martin, was climbing a ladder into some sort of garden, some sort of other territory. And . . . my father, by then dead, helps him by lifting the ladder, pushing the ladder upwards, as a result of which it falls over backwards and he [Martin] is killed.[86] [italics mine]

We view, then, a terribly ordered family, but ordered by contradiction. Under William's helm, every thing and person seemed to have its place and reason. But the overriding concern that passed between generations was the necessity to create one's own *new* order. Implicit in rebellion is continuity. Both parents and children tacitly agreed that the new order was to be one in the mind.

Perhaps the paradigm that childhood in this family offered encouraged a sensitivity for the self-negating proposition. Curiously, a magical undulation seems to have been the central rhythm of William Bateson's household. Relations, denying exactly that which they asserted, appeared to blink, coming off and turning on—like sunlight reflecting off rippling waves. If we look for pattern in the relations we have described, it is paradox that clearly recurs.

> [William Bateson's] activity was unflagging. His many varied duties and responsibilities were severally discharged as though each one was his only care. His idea of rest was change of occupation, not a lessened expenditure of energy. The only reason why people "had no time" to do any given thing, he asserted, was that they did not really want to do it.

> And certainly he found time to do very much. Unhurried and critically careful, he seemed to get through many days' work in one, and yet have time for all social pleasures. *He played as he worked, with a kind of rapid concentration of attention.* His quickness made him impatient of slowness. He could not bear to wait. Under a reserved and dignified manner lurked mirth and jollity. His intense and learned interest in life creamed over in gaiety. He was the best of companions.
>
> Very absent-minded, his pencil, notebook, knife, forceps, scissors, and even pipe (and later in life spectacles) were perpetually mislaid. Of his clothes he was a reckless school boy. He was capable of going up to London in old "garden" flannels, darned across the knee, or (in the other extreme), he might be found kneeling on the gritty garden path, in a brand-new "town" suit, recording some batch of seedlings. Such trivialities were not his affair, though on special occasions he was meticulously careful.[87] [italics mine]

The force of his character has been noted, but the substance of his beliefs seems to have been a bit tangled. William Bateson demanded that his children's education be founded on literature. He adored the poetic imagination. He had fathered a superb collection of paintings and prints. He even liked to draw. His wife recalled the following anecdote: Once, on holiday, W.B. found himself without diversion, "he had no manuscript"; they had chosen a place famous for its "absolute nullity," and soon enough, boredom set in. William, in a moment of wondrous inspiration, decided they would paint. "From that day nearly all holidays and many happy leisure hours at home were devoted to painting."[88] But though it could be deeply appreciated, though Bateson thought it to be the ultimate human achievement, and though essentially artistic intuition (inarticulate viscerality) informed the epistemology of his science, he saw that serious artistic creation was entirely beyond the Bateson gift. Thus the *one* relationship in which William was uncritically immersed was closed off to his offspring.

William Bateson's religious attitude reiterates contradiction.

He had rejected religious conviction, yet he maintained a bit of its content. The children were read the Bible at breakfast for literary purposes, and they were told to "pray" the alphabet. His system was double-edged. One could cultivate an awareness of the orthodoxy, but one's beliefs should be one's own. Traditional tenets might stir a heretical wind.

With regard to religion and art then, what William Bateson scorned he practiced, and what he idolized he forbade both himself and his children.

Bateson's attitude was that science was something one could do. It was available to the man not blessed with genius, and only it commanded total involvement (unlike art, religion, politics, and society). But his approach to science was pioneering and rebellious. It was W.B. who first termed his developing study of heredity and variation "genetics." "The old man was way ahead of his time," Gregory has said.

> He knew that the Lamarck position was intolerable anyway, that the effects of environment were not going to be inherited. . . . He knew that the internal organization of the organism was also determinative of its anatomy. . . . He was fascinated by the phenomena of symmetry and metameric regularity as exhibited by the morphology of animals and plants. It is difficult to define precisely what he was after, but broadly, it is clear that *he believed an entirely new concept of the nature of living things would develop* from the study of such phenomena.[89] [italics mine]

His contentiousness, his admiration for the individual genius, his personal isolation from the scientific community are all expressed in his advice to John, his eldest son: "The great thing is to go your own way and not to bother what other people think or say about you." Yet paradoxically, intense demands were made upon the children to continue what they saw not as science, but as their father's science. And if he had told them to go their *own* way, why did he also ask them to go his? There is the sense that they were being asked to conform to nonconformism, an impossible task at best. Perhaps something of W.B.'s personal sense of generational passage found expression in his conception of political action. "The aim of social reform," he wrote, "must not be to abolish class, but to provide that each individual shall so far as possible get into the right class and stay there, and usually his children after him."[90]

We do not know the emotional circumstances surrounding John Bateson's death, but clearly the subtleties of his father's lesson had been lost on Martin. We see him rebelliously aspiring to produce art, which, typically, W.B. had both deified and denied. Aesthetic, or heretical, or even religious Science was a possibility, but to create art, straight out, was to William Bateson much like playing God—a sacrilege—however much the gods were to be envied. And it was just this sort of paradox that killed Martin. "What I want to say," W.B. wrote Gregory after his son's suicide,

> . . . is that to people like us, work, meaning the *devotion* to some purpose, the nobility and worth of which we cannot question, is the one and only thing that helps in time of trouble. . . . *The faith in great works is the nearest to religion that I have ever got,* and it supplies what religious people get from *superstition.* There is also this difference, that the man of science very rarely hears the tempting voices and very seldom needs a stimulant at all, whereas the common man craves it all the time. *Of course, there is great work that is not science—great art, for example, is perhaps greater still, but that is for the rarest* and is scarcely in the reach of people like ourselves. Science, I am certain, comes next and that is well within our reach. . . . To set oneself to find out something, even a little bit, of the *structure and order of the natural world is . . . a splendid and purifying purpose.*[91] [italics mine]

Here, for a moment, William's science becomes religion; he is "devoted" to it, it is his "faith." But then, he quickly notes that religion for the religious is mere "superstition." Science is said to rank below art. Nevertheless, its production is "splendid and purifying." This is the convergent phrase; "splendid" connotes aesthetics, as "purifying" implies the sacred.

Thus, in its most vivid expression, we see that the father had integrated his temptations in his science. But the children may have seen them as enticements. Broadly, this was Gregory Bateson's intellectual inheritance; impelled by death and informed by paradox, it was at once uniquely flexible and ominously rigid. He had to rework it so that he might create his own position. More poetically, we might abuse a line from Blake's poem, "A Grey Monk," and describe his situation as an attempt to make ". . . a tear. . . an intellectual thing."[92]

We may now go on to weigh and judge the contribution of this inheritance to the content and style of his thought. Obliquely, Bateson seems to have commented on this very issue:

> No doubt deeper levels of the mind guide the scientist or the artist toward experiences and thought which are relevant to those problems which are somehow his, and this guidance seems to operate long before the scientist has any conscious knowledge of his goals.[93]

NOTES

1. See Gwen Raverat, *Period Piece: A Cambridge Childhood,* (London: Faber, 1952); Edmund Gosse, *Father and Son,* (Boston: Houghton Mifflin, 1965); N. Annan, "The Intellectual Aristocracy", in J. H. Plumb ed., *Studies in Social History: A Tribute to G. M. Trevelyan* (London: Longmans, Green, 1955).
2. C. Beatrice Bateson, *W. Bateson: Naturalist* (Cambridge: Cambridge Univ. Press, 1928), p. 1.
3. Personal communication from Gregory Bateson, December 27–31, 1972, Big Sur, California.
4. C. B. Bateson, p. 7.
5. Ibid., p. 2.
6. Ibid., p. 11.
7. Ibid., p. 13.
8. Ibid.
9. Ibid., p. v.
10. Ibid., p. 12.
11. Ibid., p. 16.
12. Ibid., p. 380.
13. Ibid., p. 381.
14. William Coleman, "Bateson and Chromosomes: Conservative Thought in Science," *Centaurus* 15 (1970): 297–98.
15. G. Bateson, quoted by Coleman, p. 298.
16. C. B. Bateson, p. 61.
17. Coleman, p. 300.
18. C. B. Bateson, p. 58.
19. Personal communication from G. Bateson.
20. C. B. Bateson, p. 61.
21. Personal communication from G. Bateson.
22. C. B. Bateson, p. 125.

23. C. D. Darlington, *Genetics and Man* (New York: Schocken, 1969), p. 98.
24. Personal communication from Margaret Mead, November 20, 1972, New York City.
25. Personal communication from G. Bateson.
26. C. B. Bateson, pp. 68–69.
27. Personal communication from G. Bateson.
28. C. B. Bateson, pp. 110–11.
29. Personal communication from G. Bateson.
30. Ibid.
31. Ibid.
32. C. B. Bateson, p. 61.
33. Ibid., p. 135.
34. Ibid., p. 136.
35. Ibid., p. 138.
36. Personal communication from M. Mead.
37. Personal communication from G. Bateson.
38. C. B. Bateson, pp. 148–49.
39. See Loren Eiseley, *Darwin's Century* (New York: Anchor Books, 1961).
40. Coleman, p. 266.
41. *Dictionary of National Biography*, ed., s.v. "Bateson, William."
42. *St. John's College Eagle*, April, 1926, pp. 330–31.
43. C. B. Bateson, p. 114.
44. W. B. Yeats, *The Vision* (New York: Collier Books, 1965), p. 12.
45. C. B. Bateson, p. 12.
46. C. B. Bateson, p. 97.
47. Ibid., p. 115.
48. Ibid., p. 324.
49. W. Bateson quoted by Arthur Koestler, *The Case of the Midwife Toad* (New York: Random House, 1971), p. 52.
50. Ibid., p. 51.
51. C. B. Bateson, p. 55.
52. Coleman, pp. 261–62.
53. Ibid., p. 242.
54. C. B. Bateson, p. 70.
55. Koestler, p. 54.
56. Coleman, p. 249.

57. C. B. Bateson, p. 24.
58. Coleman, p. 252.
59. C. B. Bateson, p. 138.
60. Ibid., p. 49.
61. Coleman, p. 294.
62. C. B. Bateson, p. 29.
63. Ibid., p. 24.
64. Coleman, p. 263–64.
65. Ibid., pp. 282–83. William Bateson quoted in ibid., pp. 282–83.
66. Ibid., p. 268.
67. C. B. Bateson, p. 209.
68. Ibid., p. 228.
69. Coleman, pp. 276–77.
70. C. B. Bateson, p. 422.
71. Coleman, p. 300.
72. Gregory Bateson, *Steps to an Ecology of Mind* (New York: Ballantine, 1972), p. 74.
73. Personal communication from G. Bateson.
74. Ibid.
75. C. B. Bateson p. 398.
76. Personal communication from G. Bateson.
77. C. B. Bateson, p. 159.
78. G. Bateson, *Steps*, p. 506.
79. Personal communication from G. Bateson.
80. Ibid.
81. Ibid.
82. Ibid.
83. Ibid.
84. Personal communication from M. Mead.
85. Personal communication from G. Bateson.
86. Ibid.
87. C. B. Bateson, p. 58.
88. Ibid., p. 122.
89. Personal communication from G. Bateson.
90. C. B. Bateson, p. 353.
91. Coleman, p. 298.
92. William Blake, "The Grey Monk," in *The Portable Blake*, A. Kazin ed. (New York, Viking, 1968), p. 155.
93. G. Bateson, *Steps*, p. xviii.

Daddy, Can a Scientist Be Wise?

MARY CATHERINE BATESON

Mary Catherine Bateson, linguist and anthropologist, is the daughter of Gregory Bateson and Margaret Mead. She is the author of *Our Own Metaphor: A Personal Account of a Conference on the Effects of Conscious Purpose on Human Adaptation*, which is based on a conference chaired by Gregory Bateson. Dr. M. C. Bateson lives and teaches in Iran.

DAUGHTER: What does "objective" mean?

FATHER: Well, it means that you look very hard at those things which you choose to look at.

D: That sounds right. But how do the objective people choose which things they will be objective about? . . . Which things do they leave out? . . . I mean—subjective experience shows them which things it is easy to be objective about. So, they go and study those things. But which things does their experience show are difficult? So that they avoid those things. Which are the things they avoid? . . .

F: Well, you mentioned earlier something called "practice." That's a difficult thing to be objective about. And there are other things that are difficult in the same sort of way. *Play,* for example. And *exploration.* It's difficult to be objective about whether a rat is really exploring or really playing. So they don't investigate those things. And then there's love. And, of course, hate. (*Steps to an Ecology of Mind,* 47–48)*

* Because this essay is primarily based on extracts from articles included in Gregory Bateson's *Steps to an Ecology of Mind* (New York: Chandler, 1972) and quotations from him in my own *Our Own Metaphor: A Personal Account of a Conference on the Effects of Conscious Purpose on Human Adaptation* (New York: Knopf, 1972), references to these two works have been included in abbreviated form directly in the text.

Here, then, is a list of things that the "objective people," who are essentially those who try to understand the communicational phenomena of the biological or social world (for which Gregory has used Jung's term, *Creatura*) with linear models borrowed from the sciences that focus on the physical world, the *Pleroma,* avoid thinking about. The list starts with *practice,* which is difficult to think about in the rather flattened out manner of the "objective people" because it depends on a complex structure of contexts, several logical types deep. Then we have *play* and *exploration,* which present the same sort of problem, so that the rat could perform the same, visible, physical action, and only an understanding of the entire pattern of layers of context in its behavior and relationships could sort out whether its activity was play or exploration or practice. "And then there's love. And, of course, hate." Quite true still; nonetheless, Father has definitely shifted logical types on Daughter. But after all, he is both exploring and playing.

Now it might be tempting to think that love and hate and humor (the latter is mentioned shortly thereafter), although certainly ill-understood by most psychologists, are not rigorously included in the argument that underlies the metalogue. One might think that these references appear as a sort of "throwaway line," as theater people would say. The etiquette of the well-trained reader would treat them here as almost rhetorical, but it seems appropriate to the persona my father created for Daughter in the metalogues, like the one quoted here, to see what happens if they are taken as scientific terms, and what implications this has for the nature of the argument. I'm not sure whether this is mischief or filial piety, but at any rate, I see that *love* is indexed, which suggests that it is intended not as an ornament to the argument but as a landmark in it, as are many other concepts that might be thought to be used rhetorically and turn out to have rather precise meanings, like wisdom. (Indeed, for connoisseurs of indexes, *Steps* and *Our Own Metaphor* are two of the most satisfactory books I've ever seen. Where else are Galileo, Game theory, Garden of Eden, and *Gemutlichkeit* bedfellows? Or where do Sacrament,

St. John's College, Cambridge, and Salk, Jonas, lead to Schismogenesis? In *Our Own Metaphor* we find such sequences as: *Alice*, altruism, analog coding, anthropology, Apocalypse; or homeostasis, horse training, humanness, humility, hydrogen atom.) We need to know what kind of landmarks *love* and *wisdom* are, to find our way through such diversity. Clearly, this is the "stuff as dreams are made on" and much of the problem lies in understanding the operators that relate references such as these to each other, before we can perform complex mapping activities from one type of discourse to another, and to our other worlds of thought and feeling.

Gregory himself has written about the relationships of some of these sorts of things and how they interact in the development of science. In the introduction to *Steps* he describes a diagram he once used in teaching, to try to dramatize to his students the nature of scientific thought and the shape of certain common errors. The diagram consists of three columns. In the first column, unanalyzed observations of various sorts are listed (*data*); in the second column, common types of explanatory notions in the social sciences are listed, for instance *ego, anxiety, instinct,* or *maturity*. In the third column are listed what he calls "fundamentals": truisms (like mathematics) and general scientific laws (like the Conservation Laws, or the Laws of Thermodynamics). Within this diagram, " 'Explanation' is the mapping of data onto fundamentals, but the ultimate goal of science is the increase of fundamental knowledge." (*Steps*, xxi) In the inductive methodology of much of social science, however, a different movement is involved, where new "heuristic" concepts (the second column) are developed by a study of the data. These are accumulated as "working hypotheses" and retained without being built into any sort of general or cumulative structure.

Now one of the striking things about Gregory's diagram is that the items in column three are propositions of various kinds, while the items in column two are single concepts. Whereas explanation, in relation to column three, involves mapping an observation (an event) onto a proposition, explanation as pursued through column two involves identifying some kind of causal factor. In the essay, Gregory considers the possibility that "the heuristic concepts will be corrected and improved until at last they are worthy of a place in the list of fundamentals. . . . But alas [in fifty years of work] scarcely a single principle worthy of a place in the list of fundamentals [has been produced]." (*Steps,* xix) All of the concepts in column two are the kind of thing which Gregory discusses elsewhere as false reifications. To be worthy of a place in the list of fundamentals concerned with scientific understanding of the Creatura, they would at least have to be embedded in propositions and deal with process and relationship.

Where, in such a diagram, would words like *wisdom* or *love, sacred* or *play* fit? Grammatically, they look like the items in column two. Social scientists often do take words of the language and, by modifying their definitions, insert them in column two. If we assume that these words are not being used ornamentally, we have to consider the possibility that they are being used heuristically, and that Gregory simply prefers to use the strong, old, resonating words for whatever concepts he has reached by induction. I think one would have to be of two minds about this. It is always good to read prose that sounds like English, and such words at least seem to deal with things that really matter. On the other hand, if social scientists must constantly cook up new causal principles inductively from the data, it might be better that they use terms that are recognizably jargon. Jargon allows our thinking a certain defense. Some terms are too awful to circulate freely or, when they do circulate, at least remind us of their doubtful origins. It might be a good thing if new concepts were labeled as such for a generation or so.

Another possibility, which some might regard as equivalent to the idea that such words are ornamental, would be that they enter the discussion as comments on relationship. Once when Gregory was talking to a group of specialists on cetacea (whales and dolphins), he commented, embedding that comment to his hearers in the scientific interchange, that in all our scientific discussion, because we are mammals and such things are important to us, we are discussing relationships (*Steps*, 372). Don't think it is possible, he warned, for us warm-blooded creatures to be simply objective and limited to conscious intellectuality. At the same time he is talking *about* whales and dolphins, who are absent, he is talking *with* the marine biologists. I don't think there is any question that when Gregory uses a word like *wisdom* he is at one level talking with the readers, asking us to take sides, to declare allegiances. This is part of a broader invitation that is carried by these words, to engage the emotions in the discourse. Such words as *play, love,* and *hate* refer to subjects about which it is difficult to be objective, which are nevertheless important to study and understand. Such words as *wisdom* and *sacred* remind us that we are in areas where concern and commitment are appropriate, where the deepest kind of truth is being discussed.

My own suspicion is that when Gregory uses such words, or when he intersperses poetry in the discussion, he is deliberately reaching for a double involvement of primary process and conscious thought. After all, Gregory argues that the emotions, those things that we are accustomed to regard as rather amorphous and unintellectual—indeed, as interfering with the effective pursuit of intellect—are the partial perceptions in consciousness of highly precise and patterned forms of computation. The unconscious mind *thinks*, computes, and "the heart has its reasons which the reason does not at all perceive." Emotions that enter consciousness seemingly imprecise and blurred are no more than the "outward signs of precise and complex algorithms." (*Steps*, 140) Words like *love* and *wisdom* move us. Gregory is deliberately bringing our emotions and relationships into the discussion: Perhaps we will not be confused by them, distracted from the effort to be objective, but rather will think better. Religion and art are suggested again and again in his writing as modalities which bridge the divisions of primary process and conscious thought. Seemingly in using words like *love* and *wisdom* he is engaging our emotion in the discussion and creating something like a new column to the diagram. He is inviting us to map the meaning of these profoundly significant terms—words of a special sort that have become, through art and religion, landmarks of cross-reference between primary process and conscious thought—onto the fundamentals in the formal language of cybernetics.

Before going further in examining what occurs when such words are used, and what the scientific value of that process might be, it will be useful to examine exactly what Gregory means by the two technical terms, *love* and *wisdom*.

Love

Feelings of love, emotions, are the consciously experienced aspect of precise but unconscious computations about patterns of relationship. The nearest to a definition that I can find in Gregory's words comes in *Our Own Metaphor:*

> You could say that love is a rather difficult-to-define concept, related to things we have been discussing—systems. At least a part of what we mean by the word could be covered by saying that "I love X" could be spelled out as "I regard myself as a system, whatever that might mean, and I accept with positive valuation the fact that I am one, preferring to be one rather than fall to pieces and die; and I regard the person whom I love as systemic; and I regard my system and his or her system as together constituting a larger system with some degree of conformability within itself. . . . I'm very willing to love animals, ships, and all sorts of quite inappropriate objects. Even, I suppose, a computer, if I had the care of one, because care and maintenance are in this picture too." (279–280)

When Gregory produced this definition at the Burg Wartenstein Conference, he was operating on at least two levels. He was acting, at the end of a period of stress and conflict in the conference, as a peacemaker, persuading those present to work together. Thus, he was using it in an exemplary way, inviting us to unite in a thinking system, as a conference: "Little children, love one another." He was giving us, as he said, something to work toward rather than simply fanning our respective rages about the sickness of the world. He spoke with audible emotion—slowly and painfully, with brow tense, at some length. He was also inviting us to agree on a meaning for the word. If we agreed to use the word *love* in his way, we would be entering into an agreement to accept a whole epistemology, to think in terms of systems and indeed of the hierarchical ordering of systems within systems.

The philosophical ramifications of this definition are very wide. Each of us in this view is a composite made of dynamically related parts, and as we love we potentially enter into another composite, becoming part of something larger, which is in turn part of a still larger entity, in level on level of systemic organization. Thus, from the formal point of view, my heart and my lungs love; right and left ventricle love; the members of a family love; the Browns and the Smiths, carpooling and borrowing a lawn mower back and forth, love and are members of a larger system which, to the extent that it can live at peace, loves other societies. A man and the pruning shears he holds in his hand, and indeed the tree he prunes, are parts of a system, each having parts, and together involved in the orchard and a complex symbiosis of humans and trees (and birds and insects).

All of this, however, omits the event in consciousness. There is another and contrasting meaning of love, which cuts through the hierarchies of systems and places absolute value on one particular level, the level of the individual. In that view, persons love each other and only persons are lovable. Just as the linguists have been engaged in a discovery of the sentence as virtually an ultimate unit, so Western philosophy has been involved, particularly since the Renaissance, in discovering the person, the individual, as the key level in this hierarchy of organization, the ultimate locus of value, because the person is the locus of consciousness and conscious purpose. Then in the system of man and fruit tree the fruit tree is valued for its contribution to his life, not he for his contribution to it; the parts of his body are valued for sustaining his life but could be replaced by the transplanted parts of someone else's body or by plastic; and the society is an invention for bringing about sufficient conformability between persons so that as many individual purposes can be reached as possible: the "greatest good of the greatest number" (of separate individuals). Within such an epistemology, my love and I, gazing into each other's eyes or exploring each other's bodies, find above all that our own individual personhood and identity is enhanced thereby. I am confirmed and strengthened by recognition given and also by the process of giving, but we remain fundamentally separate.

Love in the cybernetic sense has profoundly different implications from love understood in this individualistic sense. Logically, within the individualistic way of thinking, if the personhood of one is constrained or exploited in a relationship, the relationship can be discarded: The relationship has no value in itself, only the persons have value. A man and a woman, each far more than the sum of his or her parts, are themselves not a part of something which has intrinsic value: A marriage is a sort of container for their individual values, easy to dissolve, with no life of its own. Even a woman with child, living through the most profound symbiosis in the human life cycle, is not valued as a single system, what the Bible called "one flesh." We debate for legal purposes whether there are two persons (each with a soul) involved or one person (conscious and with a conscious set of priorities), and one "product of conception." If the infant is carried to term, he or she will be the concern of a pediatrician while the mother (and her breasts and milk supply) is separately defined and cared for by the obstetrician. No one will care for the system.

At Burg Wartenstein, it became clear that Gregory was using the term *mind* in much the same systemic way that he uses *love,* cutting across the person as the locus of consciousness, and focusing on complexities above and below. I wrote:

> One might almost go back over the discussions and try substituting the word "mind" for the word "system" wherever either occurred. Then "mind" becomes a property not just of single organisms, but of relations between them, including systems consisting of man and man, or a man and a horse, a man and a garden, or a beetle and a plant. Some mind-like properties seem very simple when they occur by themselves, but together they suggest a way of thinking which neither reduces mind to a model of billiard balls, nor sets it off in contrast to matter, but allows for a search through all orders of material complexity for forms of organization comparable to our own. This is perhaps a basis for a new kind of respect for the structures of the world in which we live. (*Our Own Metaphor,* 253–54)

Thus, the immanence of mind is closely related to this matter of love. Still letting the word *love* resonate, with all its literary, personal, and religious associations, it may be useful to look at the rest of that discussion of the properties of mind. (Gregory's slightly different listing of key properties occurs in *Steps,* 490.)

Mind

"Mind is immanent where there are a number of parts, moving and mutually constrained." This is of course a different way of saying that the word *mind* can be substituted for the word *system,* but it still brings out a few key issues: the issue of a dynamic relationship, of movement; the issue of constraint; the issue of mutuality. A man with a scythe is constrained by the form of the scythe; indeed his own body motion is informed by the curves of his tool, a concrete proposition about the interlocked movement of man and tool through deep growing fields across the generations; as time passes, his own musculature will become a record of the scythe's teaching, first in stiffness, then in emerging grace and skill. We need time to understand this system, to get beyond seeing it as simply instrumental.

"Mind is immanent where there are a number of parts . . . forming a system which is self-corrective, maintaining constants about the relations between the parts and relations to the environment." Certainly this is something which can be seen in families, how the entire family system adjusts to keep certain relations constant, even at very great cost to individuals within the family. That is, families in their ongoing life, both healthy families and families whose interlocking patterns of mutual exploitation force individual members into schizophrenia or alcoholism, evolve their own systemic patterns and stabilities. Families (not individuals within families but patterns of relationship) may fiercely constrain the individuals within them. Thus, perhaps the family, as well as the individuals within it, must be seen as a locus of value. Any such system may be engaged not in maintaining the constants of homeostasis but constants of continuous change, potentially destroying the parts that make it up or the larger system of which it is itself a part.

"Mind is immanent where energy is stored so that the system can be responsive to abstract cues." Here we meet our problem between man and scythe; since the scythe cannot store energy, its physical path is a direct result of the way the man wields it, albeit translated by its form. The particular scythe, unlike the peasant who wields it, cannot be thought of as a system in which mind is immanent, but mind is immanent in the system man plus scythe. He wields his scythe more swiftly as storm clouds gather or as, using the strength from his breakfast, he imagines his dinner ahead. Picking up the scythe, he becomes a part of a system. Mounting a tractor makes him part of a more complex system, complete with a gas tank.

Curiously, it is the failure to recognize the immanence of mind, to recognize for instance that the system of the man and his fields has mind, that leads to all sorts of personifications or anthropomorphizations of tools, plants, and animals, or of the very fertility of the fields. All of these so-called projections are derived from the intuitive observation that in our involvements with the non-persons we encounter in the environment, we are not alone, we are not subject and these others object, but somehow we are involved in a dialogue. Mind is present, immanent in the situation, and we have the choice between seeing ourselves as parts of a thinking system greater than either, or attributing mind to the other, often setting the other mind up as a rival and feeling bullied by the form of the scythe or sabotaged by the weather or the population cycles of "pests." It is easier to say either the tree has an indwelling spirit or it does not, either the tool has personality or it does not, either the fetus has a soul or it does not, than it is to say that all of these are terms for something which resides not in the person and (possibly) in whatever portion of his environment he is interacting with, but in the interaction. For modern man, dismissing the idea of the indwelling spirit of the tree or the soul in the unborn fetus is a way of largely dismissing them as valuable.

An odd sequence has taken place as between primary process and consciousness: Primary process has proposed the indwelling spirit as a metaphor for what is felt as real kinship between human and tree. After all, a tree is more like a woman than it is like a telephone pole, and it may be more accurate to say there is a demon in a bottle of rum than to focus on the isolated alcoholic separate from a pattern of relationship. The unconscious, in the language of art or religion, can also propose love as a proper relationship to the other. The conscious mind, however, has a strategy for this; it suggests an either-or which is quite unintelligible to the unconscious, so only a blurred intuition protests that the argument has shifted to false ground: *Either* the tree is a dryad or it is not and is not lovable, *either* the fetus has a soul or it does not—and if not, then we will not attribute value, that is, personhood, civil rights, and so on to it, and above all, we will not regard ourselves as involved in a real relationship of love. We speak of personification and the pathetic fallacy when in poetry we find ourselves forced to attribute richer being to other parts of the biosphere than our unwise conscious minds will allow. We attribute to them a similarity to ourselves partly in order to be able to love them, as part of our perception of their beauty.

Gregory's definition of *love* or of *mind* invites us to generate whole new orders of being to be valued or loved, as we perceive ourselves entering into various kinds of relationship, and thereby being changed. It suggests a sort of theogony, a new animation of the landscape of awareness.

Wisdom

As with the word *love,* to use the word *wisdom* with Gregory takes us right into the center of his epistemology. "Wisdom I take to be the knowledge of the larger interactive system—that system which, if disturbed, is likely to generate exponential curves of change." (*Steps,* 439) "Love can survive only if wisdom (i.e. a sense of recognition of the fact of circuitry) has an effective voice" since "unaided consciousness must always tend toward hate" (*Steps,* 146). The circuitry of systems is concerned with maintaining constancies of various kinds, so wisdom is essentially conservative.

From the definitions this is clear: Love entails a readiness to relate in the way that wisdom recognizes as the basic structure of the Creatura. Special experiences of self-loss, of readiness to give one's being for the beloved, of wishing it were possible to merge into a single body—these experiences are based on an accurate perception of the systemic nature of particular relationships, and yet we do not acknowledge this as the nature of all relationship. We can desire to become a part of something larger than ourselves because we know, in spite of the illusions of consciousness and the package of skin in which we move, that there is a sense in which this is how things really are. In love we encounter this as emotion; wisdom argues further—this is not the special experience of passion or dedication or self-sacrifice, this is how the world is made. Wisdom argues for love by acknowledging the kind of world in which that kind of love is the most basic experience.

Wisdom, however, differs from love in that in love our

computations of relationship can remain unconsciousness, resonating into consciousness only as emotions. Wisdom demands not only a recognition of the fact of circuitry, but a conscious recognition, rooted in both intellectual and emotional experience, synthesizing the two. Thus, "I am not sure that wisdom can be got [via drugs]. What is required is not simply a relaxation of consciousness to let the unconscious material gush out." (*Steps,* 444)

The paths that Gregory has discussed as leading to the growth of wisdom include love (and love of animals or natural systems as well as people), the arts, and religion, and these work in different ways and to different degrees. After all, contemporary society includes many highly institutionalized ways of functioning as a part person—of denying primary process, separating the body from the mind, emotion from reason, production from consumption, and Sunday from the rest of the week. Because our instructional systems emphasize only parts, they both strengthen those parts and also convey the metamessage that such divisions are appropriate. There is a sense in which any experience that breaches these boundaries brings us closer to wisdom, in which any opening to the irrational may help to complete us—whether it's an LSD trip or a fleeting experience of compassion in a boardroom, meditation or trying to carry on a conversation with a four-year-old. Many people discard the rational, trying to reject conscious thought, and remain unwise and incomplete in a new way. Others, however, are striving to breach the separations. A few go further and are working at synthesis, either by spiritual self-disciplines or through the disciplines of the arts or, occasionally, in science. Wisdom is not simply an experience, but neither is it the sort of thing that can effectively be passed on in the language of scientific papers and monographs unless these are such as to evoke a visceral as well as an intellectual response. Wisdom is the conclusion to a many-layered process of cognition at all levels of mind, and this is why the traditional spiritual ways are marked so often by paradox, the experience of dissonance between levels, which must be transcended.

Wisdom, curiously, as a recognition of the nature of the system created by participation, is equivalent to systemic self-consciousness. When human beings, participating in larger systems of mind that do not stop at the boundaries of skin and sense receptors, know themselves as a part of mind rather than as individuals, they have arrived at wisdom, whatever language they may use for that recognition. Equally, however, one might say that the system of which they are a part has arrived at wisdom: Human consciousness is potentially the organ of self-knowledge for the entire ecosystem.

Love, mind, wisdom . . . although it is not apparent every time Gregory uses them, these are nevertheless precisely defined terms in his epistemology. At the same time, however, they have an evocative impact that goes beyond our grasp of the meanings of his definitions. The us of a word like *wisdom* or *love* in an essay on the conditions of human survival invokes a whole spectrum of artistic and religious traditions, summoning to our intellectual discussions Jesus, Pythagoras, and Buddha. Thus, we are approaching the area of the sacred, which is also a technical matter in Gregory's writing, and indeed the sacramental as well.

Basically, these words, like the Old Testament name of God, Yahweh, are words of power. Rabbinical scholars knew that some things cannot be talked *about,* for the name of God partakes of His very being. Similarly, we feel that words such as these should only be used by one who—in some measure—has experienced them: Let only lovers speak of love, and let psychologists speak of object cathexis. There is a potential of both ritual and poetry in such words, and thus they are sacred words (or words for thinking about the sacred) in Gregory's sense: "It is my suspicion that the richest use of the word 'sacred' is that use which will say that what matters is the combination of [conscious thought and primary process], getting the two together. And that any fracturing of the two is, shall we say, anti-sacred. In which case, the Roman Catholics and the Protestants of the fifteenth century were equally anti-sacred in their battles [about the nature of the Eucharist].

The bread both is and stands for the body."[1] This is actually a part of the technical definition of a sacrament by the Council of Trent: "A sacrament *effects* what it *signifies*."[2] If I am right about the way such words resonate at different levels of our minds, using them is either a terrible presumption—a blasphemy—or it is an essentially hieratic act. But after all, Gregory is trying to effect what his words signify, is trying to produce wisdom and the possibility of love.

There is at present in Western civilization a new kind of emphasis on the disparity between primary process and conscious thought. At first, with the hippies and the early drug culture, there seemed to be a sort of replay of the Romantic Movement, with its revulsion against science and the effort of objectivity. However, many new elements have been added, especially the discussion of differences between the two sides of the brain. Science tends to look like an exclusively "left brain" activity, and yet any consideration of scientists as people shows that the best of them rely heavily on intuition. There is merely a formal convention in the modern publication of scientific results that filters out all that is not cut and dried, replicable and objective. In school we learn about Newton the physicist, not about Newton the religious mystic, about the experiments which confirm hypotheses rather than about the leap of questioning or perception from which they are born.

This arises from the fact that most people have models of scientific activity which are based on physics, the study of the Pleroma "in which events are caused by forces and impacts," (*Steps*, 462) and in which all that we are trying to understand is radically different from us and from our way of perceiving and understanding it, in that there are no *differences* in the Pleroma, for differences are all that we can respond to (see, measure, record, weave together as scientific knowledge). Physical science is predicated on conceptualizing what is being observed as totally separate.

I remember once talking to my father about the difference between the studies of dolphins done by people who came in to the field from marine biology and those he hoped to do. The marine biologists came from the study of organisms sufficiently simple so that scientists could have little direct empathy with them. What he hoped to do, coming in from anthropology, from trying to think scientifically about the Balinese in the 1930s or the schizophrenic patient in the VA with whom he spent hundreds of hours in the 1950s, was to use empathy in a scientific way. "They fall in love," he said of his colleagues, "they get seduced by the dolphins and they can't think straight." There are, of course, the "objective people," thinking about dolphins or Balinese or schizophrenic patients in a flattened way that avoids, among other things, awareness that there are at least two levels to be studied all the time, dolphin events, relationships, and meanings, and events, relationships, and meanings involving scientist and dolphin. The methodology combining these in the social sciences is called "participant observation" and requires what Margaret Mead was probably first to speak of as a "disciplined subjectivity" rather than a pretense of objectivity.[3] The problem is *not* to resist falling in love. The problem is to fall in love and be the wiser thereby (yes, *wiser,* in Gregory's strictly technical cybernetic definition), although anyone trained, as Gregory was, in a classic tradition of Western science treads this path a little gingerly. Nonetheless, he has premised years of study of precise but unconscious patterning on the notion that primary process is, precisely, thought. Science, if it is to make headway in thinking about the Creatura, should have the benefit of primary process computation. "Oh dear," said Daughter in the metalogue on instinct, "those poor people. They try to study animals. And they specialize in those things that they can study objectively. And they can only be objective about those things in which they themselves are least like animals. It must be difficult for them." (*Steps,* 48) Difficult indeed! It's a depressing thought that we depend so much on scientists who, if we are to believe the split-brain people, spend their time desperately trying to use only half their brains (and in fact only succeed in using a fraction of that). One would as soon depend for one's decisions on oracles and prophecies produced in trance, carrying only the other kind of knowledge. Not, in either case, wisdom.

I think we are a very long way from an understanding of the kind of scientific activity that will lead to wisdom, but a keystone of Gregory's use of cybernetics is that among the translations and analogical mappings it makes possible is a re-statement of the lucid computations of the heart. Thus, it is essential that *love* and *wisdom* and *sacred* have cybernetic meanings. At the same time, Gregory writing or speaking is never only talking *about* these issues. He is also using these evocative words to mobilize in his listeners that reasoning of the heart that the reason does not perceive. He is inviting one kind of synthesis and at the same time activating our intuitions to engage them in the scientific process. In using cybernetic definitions of love and wisdom, he is mapping what we at least partly know at the primary process level onto the scientific fundamentals, which is a way of confirming science in wisdom. A scientist, after all, like a sacrament or a poem, "should not mean but be."[4]

NOTES

1. Gregory Bateson, "Ecology of Mind: The Sacred," *Loka: A Journal from Naropa Institute,* ed. Rick Fields (New York: Doubleday, 1975), p. 25.
2. H. Denziger, ed., *Enchiridion Symbolorum: Definitionum et rationum de rebus civii et morum,* 33rd ed. (Freiberg, Germany: Herder, 1965), nos. 1606, 1639.
3. This term was developed by Margaret Mead during the Adolescent Study directed by Caroline Zachary in 1934–35.
4. Archibald MacLeish, "Ars Poetica," *Modern American & Modern British Poetry,* Louis Untermeyer, ed. (New York: Harcourt, Brace & Co., 1955) p. 272.

Gregory Bateson and Humanistic Psychology

❂ ❂

ROLLO MAY

Rollo May, psychoanalyst and humanist psychologist, is the author of many books, including *The Meaning of Anxiety*, *Man's Search for Himself*, *Love and Will*, and *The Courage to Create*. Dr. May lives in Tiburon, California.

In the spring of 1975 a group of us held a conference in Tucson, Arizona, on the topic "Theory for Humanistic Psychology." On the assumption that what we needed was a cross-hybridization of thoughtful persons in different disciplines, and knowing Gregory Bateson's capacity for elucidating the interface of these disciplines, we invited him to be one of the twenty members of the conference. What we sought was a new paradigm for humanistic psychology, a new set of metaphors, a new underlying structure. I believe Bateson's contribution to this new theory was and will be great. When the invitation came to contribute a chapter to this volume I seized the occasion as an opportunity to explore Gregory Bateson's thinking, with the aim of identifying as best I could his contribution to a much-needed theory for humanistic psychology.

In a letter to me after the conference Gregory Bateson wrote, "I do not know whether I am a humanistic psychologist; but how can the truth ever be antihumanistic?" What strikes us in this sentence is not only the part that we would agree with, that the truth can never be antihumanistic; but also that curious use of the word "truth." This word is rarely used as a general noun in these days of cynicism and relativism, when no one presumes to arrive at "the truth" as such. It would be, I felt, an enthralling project to study the thinking of someone courageous enough to speak of "truth" as such.

Gregory Bateson is also recognized as one who perpetually pushes back the barriers of the different disciplines, analyzing in the process the common emphases that these disciplines share, whether these common emphases are known by the workers in the disciplines or not. He speaks first of all as an anthropologist (which I take in the European sense of one who studies mankind rather than in the American sense of the preoccupation with primitive cultures). But we value him here especially for his interdisciplinary emphasis.

I

We may get clues to understanding Bateson by comparing him with that most original of American psychiatrists, the late Harry Stack Sullivan. Both came from the British Isles, Gregory directly from England and Sullivan from Irish stock. Both had a penetrating sense of humor and an impressive gift for language; both were fascinating talkers and were at their best in direct conversation. Each tended to get lost in the circumlocution of writing. Each was often cast in the role of Peck's bad boy at conferences (whether they chose the role or not); and the experience of having someone who revealed the group's pet biases was generally very stimulating indeed.

Their ideas are curiously similar. Both questioned sharply the American overemphasis on the individual. Both were preoccupied with communication. Both emphasized relationship, Bateson at almost every point in his theory and Sullivan in his total view of psychiatry, which he defined as "the biology of interpersonal relationships." Both—as Bateson interjected with a wry smile when he and I were discussing this—were a "little schizophrenic." Both made original contributions to the treatment of schizophrenia: Sullivan in his whole system and Bateson in his formulation of the double bind as well as other penetrating concepts relating to schizophrenia. Sullivan, says Bateson, was too much of a poet to be a formalist. The same thing could be said of Bateson.

Both took their stands on the side of the humanity of the schizophrenic patient. Psychiatrists have been generally concerned with helping the schizophrenic accept the compromise of getting along in society. Most people obviously accept that compromise, and are therefore judged "normal." The schizophrenics often cannot accept the compromise without radical inner loss—which is why they are judged schizophrenic. Sullivan sided with them, as Bateson does. One time Bateson and Sullivan met at a conference: They had both slipped out of the meeting and found themselves sitting next to each other on a stairway in a hall. There they agreed that "what happens to human beings should not happen to dogs." Sullivan, says Bateson, had a rage against those who try to adjust the individual to the culture. He protested against "man's inherent vulgarity," which could as well be said of Bateson.

Every exegesis of Sullivan I have found difficult to understand. The same is true of Bateson. I warn the would-be reader of difficult terrain ahead. But there are rich rewards for the ones who take the trouble to go into Bateson's mind.

II

Bateson begins one of his essays[1] with what he calls a little experiment for the audience. He asks the listeners, "Do you see me?" When they answer yes, he points out that they do not see him at all. What they see is a "bunch of pieces of information" about him which they synthesize into the picture of a speaker named Gregory Bateson.

This leads us immediately into the heart of the very important topic of Bateson's epistemology. He states that we create our world in that we look out at the universe through our own presuppositions, our own premises, our own expectations. We sift what we see through our own special meanings, opening ourselves to some interpretations but blocking out others which make us uncomfortable. The story is told of a tribe living on a South Pacific island who, when Captain Cook's ship sailed into their harbor, did not see the vessel because they had no word for such a ship.[2] They probably did see something like "clouds" or "an extraordinarily large bird."

Language is only one demonstration of the way our thought processes determine our perception. There are an infinite number of ways of seeing reality; we know only ours and we blandly assume, as everyone automatically does, that ours is the only way. It is in this sense that we create our own world. This is not a moral problem but an unavoidable concomitant of being human. The moral question emerges only afterward, and it is whether we will recognize our own perceptions as being partial, or dogmatically insist that other people accept our perceptions only.*

This approach in epistemology Bateson shares with the phenomenologists. He has, however, shied away from fully working out his relation to the phenomenologists, partially because of the way he sees *his* world. He feels the phenomenologists, in their concept of perception, cut themselves off from their own roots. He believes sense organs can receive only news of differences. If true, this means that phenomena are not perceived "in general" as the phenomenologists usually imply, but only when they specifically differ from something else. This would mean that the phenomenologist would have to specify what *difference* there is in the sight he perceives to cause it to register in his perception. I should have preferred, however, that Bateson work out his real relation to the phenomenologists, since they are distant cousins at the very least.

Bateson's epistemology has led some questioners, including me, to ask whether he is a Berkeleyan idealist since he holds that the only ideas we can know are those that are in our own minds. Bateson answers this query mostly with agreement. But with him this position by no means implies that there is no

* "For me," says Bateson, "the moral question is *which* of my premises I shall be dogmatic about. True, many premises are culturally relative—some are, I believe, both wrong and pathogenic. Alas, the culture can foster premises of this last kind!" (In private conversation.)

reality except the subjective one: The Vietnam War is still wrong, and our common problems in contending with overpopulation and ecological threats are starkly real. What Bateson seeks is not a philosophical relativism; he insists on an awareness of our own inescapable biases, our own parochialness. He would have us always hold ourselves open to the possibility of altering the context through which we perceive reality. It is Bateson the anthropologist who speaks at this point and it is indeed fitting that these cautions should come from that discipline.

As Sullivan found out before Bateson, what is needed is some form of "consensual validation," some bridge to others so we can escape the complete isolation and loneliness of the perpetual separation of our minds from others' minds and from reality. Some three centuries ago the philosopher Leibnitz, in his lonely doctrine of the individual monads which have no doors or windows to anything else, argued that there exists in the universe a preestablished harmony; but nowadays we have no God to insure such a harmony or to establish the parallelism of mind and body.*

This bridge to others must consist of some form of relationship. Hence Bateson has been centrally concerned with relationship by means of communication in animals and in human beings, as can be seen in the title of one of the books of which he was coauthor, *Communication: The Social Matrix of Psychiatry.*[3] As is brought out in this book, the study of communication is one scientific approach in which all of the phenomena of intrapsychic and interpersonal relations, including values theory and data from cultural anthropology, can be studied together.

One aspect of Bateson's epistemology that is especially significant for humanistic psychology is his emphasis on communication in which *validity depends on belief*. The validity of principles of ethics and aesthetics are cases in point; that is,

* A sentence of Bateson's, stated as we discussed this point, is interesting: "The objection to the words *mind* and *body* is already an idea or aggregate of ideas."

the validity of any proposition of ethics and aesthetics depends in part upon the actions and psychic state of the communicators. But the statement that validity depends upon belief is also true in many other areas, as shown, for example, in Rosenthal's demonstration of "experimenter influence." In science this is the effect on the results of the beliefs of the one performing the experiment. Taking three groups of graduate students, Rosenthal gave the first group a bunch of rats which he said were unusually bright; to the second group he gave rats which he said were especially stupid; and to the third group he gave rats about which he said nothing at all. The students were then instructed to run the rats through the maze. The rats of the first group did unusually well, those of the second group did especially poorly, and those of the third group did average. Actually, all the rats were of random intelligence.

This phenomenon is much more subtle than simply "I find what I set out to find." Are there some subtle factors in the voice and/or gestures of the experimenter which are picked up, even by creatures like rats? Or is there some ESP factor at work that is as yet unknown? Rosenthal is not certain, but he is now doing his studies with movie cameras to ascertain the differences between the attitude and gestures of the experimenter who believes his subjects are bright and the experimenter who thinks his subjects are stupid. In other words, what is the effect of the beliefs of the experimenter on the subject? Expanding the conclusion, what is the effect of the parents' believing in the child, or the effect on a friend of one's confidence in that friend? This certainly is a demonstration, on an ever-widening scope, of the phenomenon that values are partially constituted by the belief of the person in them.

These studies indicate that we, the experimenters, are bound together with those we are experimenting upon in webs far more intricate than we even begin to imagine. One implication is that the terms *subject* and *object* are obsolete. Another implication is in the question, Can we assume that our lying to the person we are studying does not in some way influence the experiment? Is this lying not bound to be picked up in subtle ways by the "victim," not consciously but subconsciously? I propose the hypothesis that the subject will know that we are lying even though he may not *know that he knows it.* He has been socialized, acculturated; he cooperates with us enough to pretend that he doesn't know. He is also awed enough by the power of "science" to play along with the experiment, as we expect him to do. My own experience in psychotherapy, like Freud's, demonstrates beyond doubt that the client or patient on some level senses a lie when the therapist tells one. All of us who do therapy have had many experiences of the patient's catching on when we prevaricate, which revelation may come out, for example, in subsequent dreams. Freud says that he draws from this a moral reason for assuming ESP, since the patient will see through whatever lies he tells anyway.

But my heart sinks when I realize that the majority of experiments in psychology, from Rosenthal's instructions to Stanley Milgram's Eichmannesque experiments to B. F. Skinner's "faking it," hinge in some way on impressing an untruth on our subjects. What does this do to the context of the experiment? Does it not confuse and change the whole context? Is such prevarication compatible with respect for the human being whom we are studying? These and a number of similar crucial questions I can only cite here.

III

If each of us perceives his or her own world, the door seems open for an excessive individualism. The concept of individualism has become a central tenet of Western mythology since the Renaissance and has held an especially strong position in the American folk religion of capitalism. When an article by me was published in newspapers around the country pointing out that the American myth of individualism, among other myths, was undergoing radical change and would die, I received a number of letters and copies of newspaper editorials politely disagreeing with that particular point in my article.

The American faith in individualism, my correspondents stated, would never change. The fact that the majority of people in this country have no objection to the government's bailing out bankrupt banks (run by individuals), but find themselves very anxious at the proposition that the government do the same for New York City (run as a collective) shows how religiously we cling to our anachronistic faith. There can be no doubt, however, that in these days of the welfare state, the growth and influence of Buddhism and other Oriental forms of emphasis on the no-self and the denial of the ego, that a movement correcting our excessive individualism is surely in progress.

Bateson—like Sullivan before him—attacks the concept of individualism in this excessive form. Sullivan wrote on the topic "The Myth of Individual Personality." Bateson points out the absurdity and arrogance of believing one is "captain of his soul" or "master of his fate." At the conference in Tucson he startled the group with the statement "I have never made a free choice." He described himself as being like a cork carried along on the current of the stream. As I understand it, this was a dramatic way of illustrating what he felt were the errors of our excessive individualism. E. E. Cummings, he points out, uses lower case for pronouns in order to avoid precisely this tyranny of the individual. To Bateson the biologist, there is a particular weight in the demonstration that the frog's leg takes its particular form not from an inbred teleology but from the frog's immediate world; that is, which side of the leg becomes the upper and which the lower depends upon which side of the frog's body the leg is grafted onto. What must always be considered is the surrounding world—the gestalt, the environment; this for Bateson is crucial to the understanding of the development and behavior of the organism. Survival for the organism consists in meeting the challenges set by the world in which it finds itself.

The interdependence leads us to one of Bateson's favorite terms, namely *context*. The first time I ever met Gregory Bateson was at Mills College, where he was a member of the discussion panel at a lecture I delivered. After the lecture the audience and I were arguing back and forth, as fruitlessly as is generally the case, about how freedom develops in the child in America. Gregory roused himself on the platform to volunteer, "The child develops freedom in the *context* of the family." Since then I have found the word *context* emerging in all kinds of forms in Bateson's thinking.

Form, order, pattern—these are terms that one finds cropping up continually in Bateson's writing and speech. He does not like to classify data in anthropology under the customary headings of sex, religion, family, and so forth; rather, he prefers to classify human beings in terms of the forms of their relationships. Do they relate to each other symmetrically, unilaterally, longitudinally? This makes the business of deriving abstract statements easier, and is to my mind a more useful and real approach. It goes below the categories of "business" or "social function" and other more or less artificial roles, and emphasizes human beings in their geometrical relation to each other. Thus the form, pattern, and order are genuine realities for Bateson, for they underlie both the *ways* of relating and the *changes* occurring in the relationships. These forms, order, or patterns are not materials; they emerge not as given substances but they are the *relationships* of things. These forms are the metaphors by which the persons are understood.

Bateson becomes unconsciously poetic when he talks about form and order, for they are touchstones of life for him. This can be illustrated in a section from one of the tapes of our conversations, which I here render in poetry because that is the way it impressed me as it came from Gregory's mouth. Gregory was speaking about patterns,

> . . . which, in the book I am trying to write
> I call my Old Friends,
> Being those patterns which I've met with before
> And shall meet with again

And which tell me that things are alive. . . .
These patterns exist in the morphogenesis of marigolds,
They exist in the morphogenesis of forests,
They exist in the book I'm trying to write,
And in any debate among clusters of people.

They are the necessary outward and visible sign
Of the system being organized . . .

IV

The importance of context in Bateson's thinking is seen also in his learning theory. The first in his logical categories of learning is "Zero Learning." The person simply absorbs more facts, more simple information. There is no progress and no change. Zero Learning is shown in habituation. There is "no new habituation, only the pre-existing habitual response to the information which is received into pre-existing known categories of meaning." Information in Zero Learning expands only arithmetically. The computer falls into this category. In Zero Learning no error and no creativity is possible.

The second category he calls, somewhat to the reader's confusion, "Learning One." This is learning when one has progressively more cues to fit facts into, and hence one's learning expands geometrically. This is learning *of* habituation, that is, one is aware of one's habituation. One acquires new connections between "stimulus" and "response" but always in familiar patterns of connection. There are no new patterns of connection. Rote learning is of this sort. Most of what we call learning in psychology also is of this variety. One is aware of the context markers, but the context itself does not change—this latter is the important thing.

The third level, "Learning Two," is learning "propositions about contexts." Now the context itself changes. The premises on the basis of which one learns now shift. Contexts which are new to the learner may induce such learning. One "learns to learn" in a new way. An example is transference in psychoanalysis, when the context (the background, the screen against which one is learning) and all of the facts one has learned take on a new meaning.* This is the changing of the "context" in which change one sees the facts in a new light. People can avoid this learning—that is, they can cling to the old "context"—by hallucination or repression. Experimental neurosis in animals occurs because the animal cannot change the "context" which it has already learned.[4]

The fourth level, "Learning Three," occurs in such things as religious conversion or in Zen experience. "When there is a contradiction of 'contexts,' Learning III may occur and be the discovery that all that pain and joy of fitting one's self to the perceived world was premised upon personal perceptions of the world . . . a system of 'glosses.' Or perhaps some other discovery about glosses."† The context as a matter of fact may be somewhat fluid. Learning III may involve a oneness with nature, or an identification with what one is learning. As in *Zen and the Art of Archery*, one's being is identified with the arrow and the target, and thus one can hit the target in the dead of night. There is an absorption in life in a new and different way. This seems to require a kind of eruption of the unconscious, that is, some kind of conversion.

There is a fifth level, "Learning Four," which Gregory Bateson says human beings perhaps never attain. I then asked him why he puts it in. He assured me that it was to keep the learning categories open-ended, and to indicate that his learning theory takes in not just human beings but the whole of nature.

* Gregory Bateson's own words about transference: "The analysand brings to the analysis old ways of perceiving a relationship to a senior male. He perceives and acts to the analysis in terms of this old (now obsolete) Learning Two. By 'analysis of the transference' he is pushed to replace the old Learning Two with a new Learning Two, and to discover *about* Learning Two."

† Bateson's comment on this section is interesting: "Yes, I agree that there is always a slippery ambience between context (as it *is*) and 'context' as it is perceived to be. Change in the latter is Learning II."

V

A crucial part of Bateson's thinking, which will be welcomed by humanistic psychologists, is his sharp attack on the common illusion in our age that science consists exclusively in amassing empirical facts, in which process one automatically discovers some new law. This is the so-called inductive method. Bateson states categorically, in his essay entitled *The Science of Mind and Order,* "I believe that it is simply not true that the fundamentals of science begin in induction from experience. . . ."[5] The reason for our confusion is that students are "trained to think and argue inductively from data to hypotheses, but never to test hypotheses against knowledge derived from deduction from the fundamentals of science or philosophy."[6] As a result:

> About fifty years of work in which thousands of clever men have done their share in the behavioral sciences, have, in fact, produced a rich crop of several hundred heuristic concepts but, alas, scarcely a single principle worthy of a place in the list of fundamentals.
>
> It is all too clear that the vast majority of the concepts of contemporary psychology, psychiatry, anthropology, sociology, and economics are totally detached from the network of scientific fundamentals.[7]

Such concepts provide a rationalization for avoiding ultimate questions. But if Einstein had not disturbed his colleagues with ultimate questions, we would have had no theory of relativity; and if Heisenberg had not asked ultimate questions we would have had no quantum theory. Bateson points out, following Molière, the absurdity in doctors' holding, as they used to, that the reason opium puts people to sleep is that it contains a "dormitive principle." Such reasoning "must always lead to something like the present state of the behavioral sciences—a mass of quasi-theoretical speculation unconnected with any core of fundamental knowledge."[8]

What has gone wrong? What is the source of the confusion? Bateson illustrates his answer with the word "energy." "Psychic energy is an inadmissible metaphor derived from a physical abstraction," says Bateson. Referring to a power in physics and engineering, it can be measured. But the term is then bootlegged into psychological thinking to refer to "strength" of emotions or "vigor," or the opposite to "fatigue" or "apathy." We speak of the energy of loving or hating, and of the transformation of energy from "genitals" to "love," blithely unaware that we are jumping from one realm to a radically different one. Freud was guilty of the great error here, but it was an error which only came out of the assumption all of us tend to make automatically in our time.

Behavioral or emotional energy is very different because it arises from our relationships. Freud was actually referring to disturbances in relationships. As Sullivan said, such disturbances arise in the interpersonal web. Bateson himself found in his research, which led to the theory of the double bind, that the source of what is called schizophrenia could arise from discontinuities in relationships. In current research with the family we continually see the difficulties that arise from confusion in relationships.

A recent egregious example of the error of carrying over a physical abstraction to the psychic realm is the use of the word "stress." This term is derived from engineering and physiology and is often used as a synonym for anxiety. Since stress in engineering can easily be measured, the hope was that it (and thus anxiety) could likewise be measured in psychological phenomena. But the crucial fact is that stress in a bridge arises from tons of weight, a material fact, whereas in human anxiety stress is due to disturbed relations with other people or to one's own lowered self-esteem, or to loneliness or lack of love. All of these latter data are relational phenomena.

A caveat from our academic psychological colleagues would be, "But using such terms as *stress* and *energy* enables us to control and predict." Bateson has a simple answer for that: "Prediction is a rather poor test of a hypothesis."[9] Many things can be predicted but that does not mean that we know what we're talking about when we predict them. The typical practice of a physician, for example, in which profession predictions are pragmatic, can well be called a "bag of tricks" and adds nothing to the fundamentals of science. At one point Bateson speaks of the "destructiveness of sheer rationalism in science."

Most experimental and academic psychology seems committed to dissecting the behavior of the organism and then treating the parts as though they were real in themselves. It is a divide and conquer strategy. But "Lord help you if you think the parts are real," expostulated Bateson in one of our conversations. The context—the relationship, order, form, and pattern—are destroyed in the process. No wonder we end up with an inert body of a once-human being, the human being having taken flight in the meantime; and we add insult to injury by offering up this inert carcass as an example of the human species.

The crux of the problem lies in the ancient dichotomy between form and substance. Freud and others in the psychological tradition made the bridge—and assuredly a bridge was necessary. But Freud constructed the bridge according to *substance* when it should have been constructed according to *form*. Behaviorists or humanists in psychology, we tend to omit form in this dichotomy, though there are outstanding exceptions like Kurt Levin. When Bateson states that induction is insufficient for science he adds, "It is at least equally likely that dichotomy between form and substance was an unconscious *deduction* from the subject-predicate relation in the structure of primitive language."[10]

Let us consider this point. The subject in primitive as well as present-day language is the *substance, what* you are talking about. The predicate is the form, the pattern, the movement, the nonsubstantial aspect. The form refers to process in contrast to substance. As we have said, words like "apathy," "fatigue," and so on refer to relationships, to nonmaterial concepts. Mental processes, like ideas, communication, organization, pattern, order are matters of form rather than substance. The myth of creation in the Book of Genesis is a good example. The passage in Genesis deals at length with the problem of the first order; it refers to the bringing of form into the void, the creating of light and the ordering of day and night and ocean and earth. It is not at all concerned with the origins of matter but rather with separation, difference, and so forth.

We must make a *pincers* movement in science, a dual approach. Bateson is fond of quoting Pascal's sentence, "The heart has reasons that the reason knows not of." What is required is vision, imagination, leading to the presuppositions by which we conceive of fundamentals and from which we deduce our order. Pythagoras saw form, order, and pattern in the universe as mathematical; he described this form in terms of triangles and rectangles. Hence Bateson regards him as a kindred soul and refers to him with considerable respect.

Bateson's emphasis at this point, like the emphases above, is that we need to understand better our own presuppositions, our own assumptions. The role of the human being is more important than we have assumed in the forming of scientific data. For example, we should say not that we discover a law, but that we *invent* one. Newton *invented* the law of gravity, Bateson states in one essay.[11]

VI

The method we have seen Bateson developing now pays off in giving him a richly fruitful avenue for understanding art.[12] Art, he proposes, is part of "man's quest for grace." Grace, in turn, he defines as a level of integration, the person with grace being the one who speaks and feels out of an integrated center. It is important to note that this integration is not arrived at by conscious, rational purpose; indeed, too much emphasis on conscious purpose can lead to a "monstrous distortion" of integration and a lack of grace.

> Unaided consciousness must always tend toward hate; not only because it is good common sense to exterminate the other

> fellow, but for the more profound reason that, seeing only arcs of circuits, the individual is continually surprised and necessarily angered when his hardheaded policies return to plague the inventor.[13]

Again, he writes,

> . . . that mere purposive rationality unaided by such phenomena as art, religion, dream, and the like, is necessarily pathogenic and destructive of life; and that its virulence springs specifically from the circumstances that life depends upon interlocking circuits of contingency, while consciousness can see only such short arcs of such circuits as human purpose may direct.
>
> That is the sort of world we live in—a world of circuit structures—and love can survive only if wisdom (i.e., a sense of recognition of the fact of circuitry) has an effective voice.[14]

Art has its function in the correcting of "a too purposive view of life and making the view more systemic."[15]

Art can do this because it arises from a synthesis—or a dialectical relationship—of what Freud called *primary* and *secondary* processes. Primary process is prelogical; it is shown in fantasy and in dreams. As its name implies, it comprises those functions that are present in the infant before discrete, logical, critical consciousness is developed. This latter is secondary process. Primary process reflects the rounded circuit; it perforce deals with the responses of the organism as a whole. It is reflected in the Catholic Church more than the Protestant; the belief in sacraments not as metaphor but as reality is a reflection of primary process.

Secondary process, in contrast, emphasizes consciousness and rationality; it is more "grown up"; it involves "putting away childish things"; it is "sophisticated," "civilized." Secondary process is shown in the Protestant Church where the Lord's Supper is seen as a metaphor, more than the Catholic. Secondary process tries to sift everything through rationality;

it represents the dominance of the left hemisphere of the brain.

Bateson believes in the resurrection of primary process. He is devoted to these forms of style, this sense of the whole in human experience, this childlike rather than childish attitude, this awareness of circuitry. Primary process is a trusting of one's intuition as part of the whole; it involves living closer to nature, letting one's self be carried by the life process.

Science is sometimes thought of as essentially a secondary process phenomenon; but Bateson would not agree. The imagination, the vision, the yearning for the whole that are necessary, at least in the great scientists, are also functions of primary process. (I am reminded of the statement by Christian Gauss: "I have had my solutions for a long time. But I do not yet know how I am to arrive at them.") Throughout Bateson's thinking and speaking one sees his desire to recover the values of primary process.

Bateson's chief hero, William Blake, is a beautiful example of the thinker and poet who does not neglect the functions of primary process. He gives credit to Blake in the preface to this book as one who "knew more about what it is to be human than any other man." He knew that "Poetic Imagination was the only reality."[16]

With respect to language, Bateson writes,

> poetry is not a sort of distorted and decorated prose, but rather prose is poetry which has been stripped down and pinned to a Procrustean bed of logic. The computer men who would program the translation of languages sometimes forget this fact about the primary nature of language. To try to construct a machine to translate the art of one culture into the art of another would be equally silly.[17]

The poetic way of looking at life is the union of feeling and thinking, when one grasps the whole with immediacy, when one trusts one's intuition as well as rationality; when the two hemispheres of one's brain work together rather than separately. Art speaks from the interface between conscious and unconscious.

Art communicates things that cannot be said, that go beyond vocal articulation. In poetry it is the art that uses the language as its vehicle; the art is the form, the pattern in the language rather than the language as such. Isadora Duncan, Bateson points out, dances her communication because she cannot say it. What absurdity to think that her communication would be better if it were put into words! Everything would be there except the art, and that is what her dancing is all about. Her dance reveals the interface between conscious and unconscious. The artist keeps his communications in this realm between conscious and unconscious without manhandling them or misplacing them. He participates in both and he transcends both.

Bateson holds that the artist perceives neither "turbulence" nor "serenity" in his relation to his artistic inspiration. Rather he expresses the relation between the two and experiences the two simultaneously. *Both* serene and turbulent—that describes the artistic poise. This implies a quickened relationship, a vitality, an intensity, all of which are the hallmarks of the artist.

VII

An important criticism of humanistic psychologists which Bateson makes is that they are "so materialistic." This may be surprising to many humanists who have prided themselves on being the group which takes the spiritual aspects of human experience into the picture. Bateson is obviously talking on a deeper level than we generally consider. He holds that we tend unconsciously to assume that the material is all there is, which is shown in our use of the term "third force." This force, like "energy," is a term that is applicable to mechanics and engineering but is not applicable to human beings with their awareness and their experience of culture. Bateson says this is what makes us humanists so defensive with respect to behaviorists. In the use of terms like *force* we are resurrecting an old battle, a struggle which dates back to the seventeenth century. Our continuing this old struggle actually makes us the conservatives.

What we fail to see is the world of forms, order, and pattern. We erroneously assume that the roles are "inside" the organism, say the human being or animal. On the contrary, says Bateson, the behavior of animals arises from patterns and forms that are shaped by relations *between* the animals. Thus they are immaterial. "Difference," for example, is nonmaterial; it does not reside in either object but in the relationship between them. How would we describe the perception of the fly by the hungry frog? We might describe it in terms of the hunger drive, but this would be a description that does not do justice to the actual perception, for the fly is an integral part of this act of perception. What we can observe is that the fly moves; with the first move the frog takes aim, and the second time the fly moves the frog gobbles it up. The frog has been able to perceive the fly by virtue of its movement, by virtue of its *difference* from the environment. Without difference there is no movement and no life.

A general harmony of sameness would be a denial of life itself. There is, in this dynamic view of Bateson's, the necessity of thinking in terms of process, but also there is a suspicion of any point of view that requires general harmony and leaves out the negative aspects of experience. I have elsewhere called this the "daimonic."[18] Without going into detail here, I think that Bateson is here approaching, from the opposite end of the universe, so to speak, what I have tried to include in the concept of the daimonic. As in the following sentence, Bateson enunciates another aspect of the daimonic: In the organism's struggle against pathology, "if this pathology can be warded off or restricted, the total experience may promote creativity."[19]

We recall the statement of Claude Bernard, the French physiologist, when he yearned for the day when "the physiologist, the philosopher, and the poet will talk the same language and understand each other." This day is foreshadowed, I believe, in the work of Gregory Bateson.

VIII

I wish to add a few comments of my own on several points of Bateson's thought in relation to humanistic psychology. This is done mostly to invite the critical thinking of readers of this article.

1. First, there is the proposition that ideas can have a validity of their own. In the notorious debate between Gregory Bateson and Carl Rogers at the College of Marin, and in the letters exchanged between the two afterward, Bateson insisted that the mental content most important to the people in that hall that evening was, "It is hot in here" and "What did the speaker mean by that?" Bateson argued that Rogers's belief that most important to the people present was the "person," was an abstraction removed several times from reality. Existentially speaking, I believe Bateson is quite right: What he cites *are* the ideas present at that moment. It is another question, however, what the people will be thinking about tomorrow as they remember the meeting. I agree also that *person* is an abstraction; a smile and a touch are not, but the words *smile* and *touch* are. Bateson offers a brand of idealism based upon biology and shored up with observation and experiment all the way from the grafting on of frogs' legs to the learning of whales to the double bind of schizophrenics. This concept—that all we know are ideas in our own minds—is both shocking and refreshing. Coping with it will be a new experience for many of us and may feel like plunging into the cold Pacific at San Francisco. We do not yet know what the long-run implications will be.
2. The second point refers to humanistic psychologists' relationship to behaviorism. It is chastening to be reminded of

our defensiveness in regard to behaviorism. This defensiveness springs from an awareness that behaviorism has answers to some problems and we do not (however grossly simplistic many of the behaviorist answers may be). But also the defensiveness comes from our guilt at making the same underlying assumptions as the behaviorists—namely materialistic assumptions—much as we dislike to admit the fact. It is clear that our own presuppositions must be clarified. In the meantime the example of Bateson gives us two guideposts. One is to accept, encompass, and use behaviorism in those areas where it does fit, as in some therapy, rote learning, the value of rewarding behavior, and so forth. The second is to remain undaunted in our basic assumptions about the nature of the human being. Our original belief in humanism seems to me strongly fortified by Bateson.

3. At last there is elucidated a clear and constructive approach to science. Bateson's writing at this point should be tremendously refreshing to those of us who have often felt trapped in the scientific theories now dominant in the social sciences. In my judgment he gives us, in his criticism of contemporary social science, the caution to keep continuously aware of the fundamental questions of science. His combination of induction and deduction comprises an eminently sound approach to scientific method. Bateson demonstrates how a thinking human being can be aware of both the reasons of the heart and the reasons of the mind.
4. I need do no more than point to the value of Bateson's encompassing of art, religion, and poetry in his system, whether it is in the discussion of Genesis or Pythagoras or William Blake or Blaise Pascal. Here Gregory Bateson reminds me of the classical philosopher: I have often felt that the breed was dead, what with the overwhelming concern in contemporary philosophy with linguistics and with kibitzing on science. But in Bateson we see an example of the classical breadth along with extraordinary penetration.
5. Gregory Bateson stands at midpoint between the truths elucidated by American science and those that are part of

the wisdom of the East. I refer not only to the inclusion of Zen in his categories of learning, although this is one expression of my point. I refer mainly to his attitude toward excessive individualism and freedom. The posture of the "triumphant self" is completely foreign to Bateson. He denies superficial freedom in favor of a greater freedom. This is what Buddhism does. When Ram Dass talks of being part of everything and points out how the will can be surrendered—"not my will but thine be done"—he is expressing a concept not of determinism, but of the surrendering of simple and often picayune freedoms for a more inclusive freedom. This bridge from American science to Hindu and Buddhist thought, which Bateson offers us, has implications that are indeed far-reaching.

6. The final point is in the question, What is the relation of Gregory's concept of "form-pattern-order" to the concept of myth as shared by Joseph Campbell, Mircea Eliade, and myself? I see many similarities, some overlapping between this understanding of myth and the form-pattern-order. If you translated Bateson's "form" or "pattern" into existential living terms (that is, if you made the *logos* flesh) then, I believe, you would have a myth.* Myth is the structure that gives pattern to human events. Myth gives order, like the myth of creation in Genesis which Bateson quotes. In any case, I would hope the discussion of myth in relation to form-pattern-order, as well as the discussion of other points in this paper, will stimulate the invention of new paradigms and metaphors for humanistic psychology.

* I do not know whether Bateson would agree with this or not; we have not discussed section VIII of this paper.

NOTES

1. Gregory Bateson, *Steps to an Ecology of Mind* (New York: Ballantine, 1972), p. 478.
2. Told to me by Professor Donald Snygg.
3. Jurgen Ruesch and Gregory Bateson, *Communication: The Social Matrix of Psychiatry* (New York: W. W. Norton, 1951).
4. In private conversation.
5. Gregory Bateson, p. xxii.
6. Ibid., p. xxiii.
7. Ibid., p. xix.
8. Ibid., p. xx.
9. Ibid., p. xx.
10. Ibid., p. xxv.
11. Gregory Bateson, "Metalogue: What Is an Instinct?" in *Steps to an Ecology of Mind,* p. 39.
12. Gregory Bateson, "Style, Grace and Information in Primitive Art," in *Steps to an Ecology of Mind,* p. 128.
13. Gregory Bateson, p. 146.
14. Ibid., p. 147. I quote extensively from this chapter because Bateson says so well what many of us have thought for years but been unable to express.
15. Ibid., p. 147.
16. Ibid., p. 463.
17. Ibid., p. 136.
18. Rollo May, *Love And Will* (New York: W. W. Norton, 1969), Chapters 5 and 6.
19. Gregory Bateson, p. 278.

Some Discussion of Ethnography, Theory, and Method

❂ ❂

RAY L. BIRDWHISTELL

Ray L. Birdwhistell is an anthropologist responsible for the development of the science of kinesics, or body communication. He is the author of *Introduction to Kinesics* and *Kinesics and Context*. Dr. Birdwhistell is a professor at the Annenberg School of Communications, University of Pennsylvania, and the Eastern Pennsylvania Psychiatric Institute. He lives in Brigantine, N.J.

Teachers who listen to their students rediscover that words that have been useful tools for one generation can, and often do, become icons or cliché forms in the hands of another. While the student of language can hardly entertain the hope that particular content can be stored inside particular word shapes and remain inviolate in a changing society, sophistication about the inevitability of meaning shift is scarce protection from the feeling that there are some technical terms which should have a longer half-life than, say, a popular song or a dance step. And, even when reason instructs otherwise, there is something dismal about the process of watching concepts that took lifetimes to shape be tapped of substance. Recently I have had to face the fact that many students, including my own, are now using words such as "theory," "methodology," and, in particular, "ethnography," in a very different way from my contemporaries. I had always found myself quite clear on such matters but an incident in an advanced graduate seminar destroyed the illusion that it was other people's students who were devitalizing these terms.

The seminar had been discussing the implications of the film *Dance and Trance in Bali* and the books *Balinese Character* and *Naven,* when a student asked whether Bateson and Mead had a methodology. The other students treated the question as though it had merit and seemed uncomprehending at my "Of course not. They are experienced ethnographers and not technicians." The student who asked the question was one who could not resist the temptation to submit term papers with titles such as, "Hard and Soft Science" and "Sociology: Art or Science?" but his question seemed representative of class interests and position. Certainly his question made greater sense to his classmates than did my peevish response.

In the minutes remaining in the class I tried to make clear what was involved in the use of the phrase "*a* methodology" when talking about ethnography. I tried to clarify the idea that methodology, at least as taught and practiced by the ethnographers I have known best, is not merely a technique for eliciting information related to closed and immutable questions. Nor is it a bundle of techniques; some kind of handy-dandy tool kit prepacked for field use. With this class I had long since abandoned the word *fieldwork* or the phrase *field methods*. The "field" for them is any place outside of a library or the computer room and "field methods" seems to have become a term covering any *technique* for the elicitation of data other than that derived from a classical manipulation of variables experiment. Part of this is easy to understand. Few of the students make any distinction between technique and methodology. Most of them are very good about the difference between tactics and strategy but were clumsy when they attempted to discuss the relationship between an investigator act and the larger research plan which gave significance to that act. However, it is easy to complain. The interdependence of theory and methodology can be hidden by exclusive focus upon either philosophy or technique. Once separated, only the most sophisticated can reconstitute them into investigatory practice.

It is easy to blame the floor for breaking the dropped egg. There seems to have been a growing tendency, particularly among those disciplines concerned with what is termed "direct observation," for a number of investigators to reject the use of theory except as a device for the *interpretation* of data. Without much evidence other than the papers I have been receiving or listening to at conferences, I have come to the conclusion that the past twenty-five years have seen a growing separation of theory from methods of research procedure. This tendency becomes manifest in the choice and analysis of import of problem, in the location of observational site, in the preliminary isolation of data, in the development of relevant, consistent, and explicit techniques of observation, in the recording and storage of data, in the orientation of rules of evidence, and, finally, in the methods of data *and evidence* assessment and presentation that permit and assist in ordering reexamination and research. If one can evade the history of research and of the theories leading to and developing from it, it becomes no task at all to open a paper: "In the beginning was this experiment."

A review of college catalogs (an odious task) indicates that for the social sciences there has been a burgeoning of courses entitled "Methodology." Side by side with these has been an increase in listings in "Theory." If in this one instance the catalogs can be taken somehow to represent classroom reality, it is clear that for some, not only is method separable from theory, but seldom are method and theory allowed to meet. It seems to me that these listings represent academic advertising, designed consistently with student (and faculty) prejudices that can view theory as esoteric, philosophical, and supposed to come from the mouths of the brilliant or the elderly. Method, I was told seriously by a department head, should be taught by tough, hardheaded young empiricists. There seemed little merit in reminding this man, who relegated the methods courses to himself, that etymologically the word *empiric* was a synonym for charlatanry and that it stood for medical practice without recourse to theory. Just as did his students, this man often used the term *empirical* interchangeably with *pragmatic,* and he felt as they did that such techniques of eliciting data protected the scientist from "fuzziness," "functionalism," and, even, from "logical positivism." This may be an extreme case but it is consistent with a terminological situation in which the term *scientist* can be and often is used interchangeably with *researcher.* More seriously, the term *objective,* on the one hand, can be synonymic with *quantitative* and, on the other, may describe descriptions which contain neither adjectives or adverbs.

Obviously, even a shallow acquaintance with the literature of ethnography makes clear that there are outstanding exceptions to this broad criticism. But, and this is particularly true for the direct-observation methodologies, it is impossible to disregard the extent to which "method" can be used as a prophylaxis against the diversionary intrusions of theory. It may serve with almost equal force to reduce the likelihood of unexpected data. A clear example of such technique involves the use of quick visits to "the field," several weeks of filming or sound taping, the organization of a committee of locals (called "native informants" and later elevated to judge the data), the elicitation of comment from these through the use of a schedule, and the results of the recordings and the responses quantified and published as if data can become evidence through such procedures. Clearly there can be no objection to this assemblage of techniques as techniques. However, the material gathered *is* data and not ethnographic evidence. Such data are not, I maintain, to be employed as comparable to those gathered by more traditional ethnographic investigations. In fact, this transplantation of laboratory techniques to off-campus locations should not, from my point of view, be described as cross-cultural fieldwork, and certainly should not be seen as examples of the ethnographic method, nor the results gathered by such techniques described as an ethnography. Ethnography, as a discipline, represents a tradition of research, a field of study with a substantive subject matter, and involves a range of training. It is not merely a term for reporting exotic behavior.

Traditionally, and I use the term carefully and advisedly, for a study to be seen as ethnographic, the ethnographer needed some training (field or formal) in ethnology, and insofar as it was available, knowledge of the cultural area to be studied and its surround, social and geographic. Preferably the ethnographer went into the field with as much information as could be gotten on comparable cultural areas. Equally, if not more important, an *informant,* if used as an access to cultural values, needed to be understood in terms of the relationship the person had to the society he or she represented. Terms such as "sample" or "respondent" as used in certain types of opinion polling or as a source of auxiliary data in an experimental situation are not substitutable for knowledge about the investigator's source of data. Informants are not rats; all too often they learn in a single lesson.

For more than fifty years ethnologists and social and cultural anthropologists have sought to develop and try out carefully ordered cross-societal and cross-cultural methodologies that could secure data that would become evidence about the extent of human social malleability. An essential question for most anthropologists has been whether it is even possible to develop methods that would make cross-cultural comparisons feasible and reliable. It has been an *essential* doctrine of anthropology that no comparison can be any more reliable than the ethnographies upon which the comparisons are based. Any investigatory technique which cheapens the data enervates cross-cultural comparison. The establishment of either ranges of cross-cultural variation or human universals requires the most rigorous caution in establishing the comparability of data. One of the most serious developments in recent years has been the resurgence of the version of universalism that maintains that since any human is so similar to all other humans physiologically, there is a reduced need for the development of safeguards that would enable us to detect and comprehend the social significance of seemingly identical acts. Theory and training in cross-cultural investigation give way before the destructive assumption that however noncomparable the data, it can always be generalized significantly by statistical procedures or computer. It requires very little training to count; a very intensive training is required to develop significant units for the counting.

In trying to respond to the student's question about Bateson and Mead I was trying to explain some of the methodological influences they had had upon my own work. From my first acquaintanceship with them and with their work, they impressed upon me the importance of using recording devices as tools. Patiently, they led me from a position where I had viewed the camera and the recorder as clumsy and expensive prostheses for those with insufficient discipline to achieve literacy to one which saw these implements as technical devices that could be put at the service of methodology. In particular they gave me my initial understanding of the difference between a research document and a movie, between an investigatory and a didactic instrument. Although others may have made moving pictures of non-Western peoples that have been more successful as economic enterprises, no one has had a greater impact on the discipline than they have in legitimizing the use of the camera and recorder as *tools*. However, the legitimate use of film and tape as aspects of a larger methodology requires training, knowledge, and sophistication. In the hands of the naive or untrained, the recording instrument becomes little more than artifice or irrelevant technique. This is not meant to depreciate films designed to instruct or entertain. The films so developed may, as an artifact of their manufacture, contain research data of great value. The work of Alan Lomax attests to this.

Because the work of the editor, who is also often the camera operator, is so visible in documentaries, such films are often more useful to the researcher than are some that are products of the new "ethnography." This latter involves the use of the camera or the tape recorder as a kind of vacuum cleaner, aimed in the direction of human activity. In such records there is an inevitable shape or plot recorded as a function not of the social organization external to the recorder, but of the out-of-awareness of the camera person or sound person. Such data has the strengths and weaknesses of other data gathered by untested projective techniques. It has been said that the camera cannot lie. Perhaps a better statement is that in an alien society, a camera person or a sound person, if untrained in cross-cultural theory and methods, has no ability to tell whether he or she is telling the truth or not. I am still indebted to Gregory Bateson for his insistence thirty-five years ago that distinctions such as genotype and phenotype had relevance for concept construction as part of research into human social behavior. He made me pay closer attention to the dangers inherent in making single classes of events that looked or sounded alike and of making separate classes of events that only looked or sounded different. Perhaps, to say it differently, he sharpened my apprehensions about the incapacity of data, once recorded, to resist bad classification. Less directly, he gave shape to my conviction that when the Good Lord gave man eyes and ears, he also promised him that he did not have to see or hear. The nature of the fig leaf has intrigued me during all of my research life.

A narrow operationalism can reduce direct observation of social behavior to a sterile counting of aprioristic items wrested from their context. However, in the name of one or another of the culture-conscious contemporary philosophers, direct observation can be reduced to the most amateurish impressionism. It is not surprising that with the growth of general anthropological teaching around the world, students and their mentors from a variety of disciplines make obeisance to the role of culture in the shaping of perception and observation, and acknowledge the relevance of implicit, culturally derived logics to the investigation of social practice and social organization. The literature makes it clear that it is regarded as necessary scholarly practice to testify that it is impossible to be uninfluenced by conventionalized and habituated sensory channels of observation and review. The conviction that such apologies are largely *pro forma* is supported by the dearth of information about the observer's training or of training situations in which observation can be systematically and explicitly supervised. There are many places where the student is taught the technical use of a camera or sound recorder but almost none where the student can learn what to film or how to analyze the results of the recording. Many film or tape with the assumption that the technology of recording erases or at least insulates against ethnocentrism. The insistence that a sound camera or a tape recorder can produce "objective" data is much the same as describing the microscope as a "scientific" instrument. In a world of things, the thoughts immanent in their usage can go undetected.

The results of these observations, at times termed "randomized" and at others, "controlled," are all too often tested by vote or by meditation and when familiar scenes are studied, by a technique in which the observer uses him or herself as a "native informant." Having piously testified to the power of culture, the would-be researcher through simplistic reliance on technology often reduces the discussion of observation to the level of individual perception. Differences in the results of observation can be explained as the result of differential size of sample or of the intrusion of the observer. Most often, differences in observational ability are seen as a matter of variable intelligence or of sensitivity on the part of the observers. Gross interpretations of cultural relativism at times support an observational atomism. All observers are merged as equivalent, and observational reports are equated and generalized statistically into evidence. A comparable philosophical position can be used to treat the observations as so individualized as to be nongeneralizable. In the name of culture (in the late 1960s the word *establishment* was used) or of individual differences, the conditions and the nature of training and the review of training as related to the systematic gathering of pertinent data can be depreciated, trivialized, or most commonly, ignored.

Perhaps the most extreme form of the pseudorelativistic argument is that which precludes all systematic examination of data or of the situations derived from a manipulation of theory. Explained as out of reach, the investigation of nature becomes secondary, and avoided lest it disturb introspection. Human beings (or animals) may not be looked at or listened to or made contact with in any way *because* the observations are seen as so predetermined by categorical orientations in language and logic or, conversely, are so shaped by the peculiar experiences of the individual observer as to make the data derived through observation no more than anecdote or private reflection. Perhaps one of the reasons I reacted so strongly to the student's question about methodology was that I have deeply resented the invocation of Bateson's name by those who seek to avoid all systematic research into human or animal social behavior.

The question about whether Bateson has a methodology or not punctuated my boredom with students whom I have heard quack, "After all, it's only a matter of epistemology" in precisely the same tones and with the same paucity of content as their fathers had when they said, "After all, it's only a matter of semantics. . . ." The "only" in these sentences reduces investigation to logical manipulation, to research in isomorph juggling, and it transforms "science" into the shuffling of categories. In a sense, the results of the separation of theory from research method or of research method from theory are much the same. Techniques can preclude a methodology that can give significance beyond that which is inherent in the collection procedure. Comparably, theoretics can enervate the investigation by a nihilism that makes observation trivial if not impossible.

It is probably unfair to develop this present thesis as a complaint against contemporary usages. We are indebted to the graduate of the last ten or fifteen years for making the problems involved in the new ethnographies so manifest. It is undeniable that anthropology departments of a generation or two ago gave their students precious little explicit preparation for their fieldwork. Or, to say it somewhat differently, relatively little classroom attention was given to field techniques. I recall thinking that, by and large, a "dunking" technique prevailed in most departments: A student was stuck into the field for a period and then reprieved with whatever information had adhered to him. The fact that this system, or apparent lack of one, seemed to produce good material from time to time makes it difficult to be wholly critical of the present tendency to go into the field, aim a camera or a microphone at a social occasion, and come back with the conviction that social convention or "culture" has been ethnographically recorded for posterity.

It is easy to idealize the past and to view present training techniques with alarm. However, in a more leisurely period, the student tended to go into the field with considerably more general education than many have today. Neither the formal training period nor the field experience was governed, to the extent that it was after World War II, by the economics of grants, scholarships, and fellowships. In a number of the early anthropology departments the absence of explicit instruction in ethnographic field techniques did not result in total absence of preparation for the field experience. Steeped in the literature, the field investigators, often without being conscious of it, worked out a methodology in the field consistent with prevalent theory and adaptable to the exigencies of the field situation. Thus, what a good field worker did was neither trial and error nor rigid technical data collection. There is no need to romanticize these old days. A great amount of the data from many of the early investigations are questionable if not downright useless. The point that I am attempting to make is that there are those who can use the past as rationalization for the collection and abstraction of data without previous anthropological training and without reference to theory. Comparably, the past may be used to justify the substitution of the armchair for investigation, of training in philosophy for training in the collection and assessment of data. There are, perhaps, a smaller number who can make use of the past to gain perspective upon old data, for sustaining or modifying theories, and for developing methodological systems.

It is perhaps indefensible, if not merely old-fashioned, to say that ethnographics are done by ethnographers and that the act of filming, taping, or interviewing other people does not make one an ethnographer. I find myself able to resist the present trend of using the term "ethnographer" for any cameraman, sound recording specialist, or novelist who turns skilled production attention to exotic social subjects. I find no need to call the results of their endeavors, however skilled, ethnographic. I have boundless respect for the proficient cameraman and sound specialist, as well as for the journalist or novelist. In fact, I have so much respect for them that I do not need to depreciate their work by obfuscatory title. It is not that the ethnographer does something better than these other folks; it is that he or she does something different. And, as ethnographer, a person does it differently because of a particular intellectual background and tradition, because of a special training, and because of the particular canons of criticism that can (not "may") be legitimately applied to the work. And this latter is of paramount importance. The critical audience for the ethnographer's product, the audience to whom the ethnographer is ultimately responsible, is made up of others trained in a comparable manner. That training and experience must be sufficiently similar that the conditions of data collection and assessment are communicable. This is the critical issue. An ethnographic report may or may not entertain, it may or may not be stimulating, it may or may not be didactically efficient, and it may or may not be beautiful. The criteria for its legitimization are more explicit that those conventional for other audio-visual endeavors. The methods involved in the construction of the report must be open and available to others. In this sense, "communicable" is related to an explicit reduction of information.

It is possible that one of the reasons that some students have become confused about Bateson's identity rests in the breadth of audience to whom he seems to address most of his later writings. This, combined with the fact that Bateson did not start out as a traditionally trained anthropologist, did not choose to spend his life tutoring graduate students in anthropology, and has few publications in the official anthropological journals, probably contributes to the student uncertainty. But to be explicitly and appropriately personal, as one who as a graduate student in anthropology discovered *Naven* on his own, and who was repeatedly influenced after that by conferences, coresearch, and conversations with Gregory Bateson, I feel no confusion about his contributions as an ethnographic researcher. An ethnographer is one who, on the basis of explicitly stated theories about man and social organization, develops hypotheses (or problems or questions) in a manner which makes them investigable in a range of cultures. As an ethnographer, he or she searches for a research situation and for research tools that will implement these investigations. The research situation and the tools are developed with the full recognition that they must be *explicitly* relevant to the methodology inherent in the question and in its exploration. In his insistence on methodology as theory and on theory as methodology, Bateson, the ethnographer, influenced my own work. The fact that he has spent a greater part of his life (with a question to be investigated) in the search for the appropriate site and for the tools appropriate to that site and to that question is the important point for me. Whether the question that he has mulled has the shape of "evolution" or of "communication" is relatively unimportant. And it is important that he has resisted the power of answers or of oversimple methodologies that might have foreclosed upon his curiosity. And, it was these things that I had in mind when I tried to answer the student, first in traditional and then in more contemporary jargon.

Among the ideas that I have over the years exchanged with Bateson, taken from him, or been edified or confused by him, those relating to the natural history method have served me best. Perhaps more than any of my formal teachers, Bateson led me out of a narrow view of biology as it had been instilled by courses organized for premedical students. He early persuaded me to study the work of rigorous natural historians, to pay attention to humans or animals or social practice or to evolution as phenomena to be understood in their natural settings. In our every meeting, even though much of the detailed and necessarily minute data I manipulate often fails to excite him, he has supported my contention that communication is a social matter and that the intrusions of premature classical experimentation, of isomorphy by fiat, obscured more data than they produced. His understanding or feeling for natural setting has provided him with investigatory safeguards that have assisted me over the years in my own research procedures. I recall that Bateson was once asked what he would like to say to an animal if he ever cracked its communication code. He answered, "I'd ask that animal under what conditions, in what setting, with how many and what organization of his fellows, and what order of duration of communication would be required for him to be capable of telling the truth."

"Truth," like "knowledge," unless it is stored in "intention," is located not merely in exchanged words but in *the regularities of all shared behavior*. This is central to the conception of communication behavior as an integral and ultimately inseparable aspect of social behavior, and, thus, of social change and continuity. I believe, as does Bateson, that this is investigable. Consistent with this conviction I have for the past five years been attempting to study the social, the interactional, the communicational behavior of a variety of American fathers and children. I say "attempting" for the controls, the limitations, that will make such a behavioral study feasible are not separate from but intrinsic to the regularities, that is, the structure of relating which appears to govern the behavior. These regularities must be recognized and isolated in sufficient detail that I can plan to see and hear what I wish to observe; that, in this case, I can order the filming and taping of the repetitive social interaction I am beginning to see. I am trying within a single natural site to record and analyze the similarities and differences between several "types" of families. This makes the problem particularly intriguing. In the least technical sense, the larger field within which my field of social intercourse occurs is a ramp at the northeast tip of an island. This ramp, down which boats are launched, provides the center of the stage I observe. My families consist of fathers and/or husbands, children and/or brothers or sisters, and, at times, wives and/or mothers and various other scene members. I am not studying social roles and it is the system of interaction rather than the pattern of reciprocals that determines my focus. I am attempting to establish a situation and a methodology by means of which I can compare the Polish-American, the Italian-American, the Jewish-American, and old Main Line American family patterning I observe. (These types are self-imposed, the designation the most polite forms of the terms they call themselves and each other.)

I said above that I have been working on this problem for five years. During that time my observations have produced a great deal of data and multiples of unanswered questions about the scenes under observation. However, in another sense, this work is not a *piece* of research but a continuation of a lifetime of investigation that could be stated in the terms used in Bateson's response about animals. If I ever crack human communication, I want to ask a human—or some humans—(through whatever media we can use to make regulated contact) under what conditions, within what physical settings, with what organization of his fellows, or what order of duration of communication would be required for him to answer me truthfully . . . even if that human must teach me the question that can be so answered.

In the spirit of this attitude toward investigation I will now open a journal that was drawn up from my first field notes that ten years ago laid the groundwork for the present research. This is not an ethnography but a rumination, a reflection that emerged between two periods of organized research. I thought of publishing it once, but then there was no appropriate place to put it. Now there is. I'll share it with Bateson as he has shared his metalogues with me.

❂ ❂

BITS FROM AN ETHNOGRAPHER'S JOURNAL
(1966–68 with notes 1972–75)

It is a midafternoon tide. As the sea withdraws the sandpipers scamper, feeding on the little things and, maintaining toe-depth, advance and retreat at the wave edge. A child approaches. The sandpipers themselves become a wave, slip airborne down the beach near the gulls, who posture, pose, and threaten with one another. Locked in gull talk, they pay no apparent attention[1] either to the sandpipers who dance at the waves' edge or to the garbage-feeders who rise and fall with the swell just beyond the surf break.

Back up the beach, men and women and children move seaward to take station on the emerging sand space. Some have expanded territories taken at high tide while others migrate with the newcomers to the drying beachline, to mark new areas as their own.[2] Spread blankets, beach chairs, and umbrellas, with or without human sentinels, signal claims to area as inviolate as though fenced.[3] The footprint patterns pressed in water-smoothed sand bespeak the difference between public and private space.[4] While those with considerable paraphernalia have larger spaces, an area marked only by a folded towel or a pair of beach shoes can remain respected[5] from tide to tide.

From my window the beach seems populated by groups and by isolated people.[6] Some appear alone, rooted in the sand. Others, as I telescope my perceptions, turn slowly on invisible spits, basted, brushed, and picked at by their companions. These periodically dip their hot bodies in the surf or make a brief exhibitory[7] promenade up the beach and back. In contrast are those who spend the sun time in the water, who return to touch base before dashing back into the sea.

[1] Check behavior when no sandpipers or garbage-feeding gulls.

[2] This is questionable jargon borrowed from ethologists—implies "possession" rather than rest right or passage right or quarantine.

[3] Question "inviolate." Is "fence" here a container or a barrier? Both?

[4] In social terms what is the difference?

[5] By whom? For whom are they a challenge?

[6] Just as does "private" above—"isolated" may be the statement about self—not the situation.

[7] All display behavior needs reexamination in terms of actor-spectator negotiation and settlement arrangements. Is Goffman of relevance here?

The movement of children out from their home place makes overlapping areas that flow around but seldom enter adult preserves.[8] And yet, this is no simple ground plan with single overlay of sedentary adult and ranging child. Some children play within the family space, lean toward their parents, who lean toward them, and with their parents move down a corridor to the sea and back. Other children shift their weight away from the adults but stay within the compound, their privacy no rejection. The children play, castle-building in the sand, while the adults turn inward toward themselves. Dumbbell shaped, the area is continuous, its affairs in balance.

More visible are the few youngsters on this beach who test the afternoon away: each move a trial, the range an issue never settled. Among these, the free-agent child is rare. Extruded, he is a scout and the space he penetrates becomes a family right of way,[9] its limits set by others.[10] Other children move by parental definition.[11] Too far from base or too close to other groups, they are brought home again by adults who rise to follow and retrieve.[12] These children test within the family reach. Family matters need settling before the outer world is probed.

In many of the clusters, the adults and children seem unresponsive—of little consequence to one another. This is illusion, for, if watched, they appear attached by unseen strings to passive but omnipotent adults. A few, like kites, take all of the line they can pull out and wander free on tether before changing winds. Apparent, too, are the yo-yo children. They spend the hours bouncing to the end of their line only to roll back to the family group—to wander or be thrown out again. Secure

[8] Are there age-graded niches? If so, reexamine idea of niche as socio-biological rather than psycho-physiological?

[9] Again, what are passageways? Related to "time out"—or safe places?

[10] Other "whats"?

[11] Really? Or *as if?*

[12] Does statement of intention here obscure multifunctional, i.e., multifield, behavior?

in restricted liberty, the string a reassurance to parent and child alike, the pull of string reminder of nonloss.[13]

Coveys of adolescent[14] girls pour over the big dune to cluster and divide. Having made the scene they put it to their use. Flopping on spread blankets, they lie side by side, almost touching, and as if on sporadic command, roll in unison. Supine inactivity and parallel isolation is interrupted by brief grooming frenzy,[15] mock fights and food exchange. With no apparent regularity and by no ascertainable stimulus, individuals, pairs and, more rarely, the entire group explodes from the territory to rush in to another.[16] Additions to an adolescent territory seldom lead to its expansion; rather, only its density is affected after the first brief and mock-ecstatic greeting ceremony.[17] Periodically, a girl detaches herself and stands for a few moments, belly deep in the water, her hair protected from the wave splash.

For several of the adolescent girls, the lifeguard stand is a stop; in twos or threes they lean upon one another and upon the stand as they talk up to the whistle-blowing boy guardians of the beach. As these older girls arrive, the ten- and eleven-year-olds who maintain station before the stand drift a few yards away, watchful but unnoticed. As the adolescents leave the stand, the younger girls return. And, there they practice until, as dusk approaches, the adults break camp.[18]

[13] Interesting fantasy. Check out Chinese children and fathers in the zoo film *Microcultural Incidents in Ten Zoos.* "Nonloss"—economics or security terms? Equally dangerous.

[14] Descriptive—contrastive or insignificant?

[15] Analogy—"groom" may obscure the tactility structure here.

[16] This is worth pursuing. Dense is not number of persons but condition of organization.

[17] Distrust "greeting ceremony"—social punctuation at one level —connective–entrance fee–cross-referencing sign that calibrates shape of relationship. Greeting ceremony is an obscurationist term in that it implies *a deux* shape.

[18] Keep after the relationship between "stage" as a metaphor (observer's view) or a reality (actor's view). Is drama a metaphor of a metaphor? (Jargon question. Restate.)

As if in counterpoint to this gentle rhythm, preadolescent boys[19] swarm in continuous activity. Most of their afternoon is spent in the water, waiting and riding the waves, their rubber rafts cutting close to but seldom hitting either the adults in the deeper water or the little children[19] who play in the knee-deep end crest. A few dig grave-sized holes. There is no pirate treasure, but it is they who cut through the laminae of oil sand left, their parents' lifetime before, by sunken oilers. They ignore the little ones except to shift, to shield the elaborate edifices they fashion with wet dribble sand.[20] An outgoing tide leaves them the right to destruction and in a spasm of kicking, the territory is returned to public domain.[21] The beach restored, they break to swim or skim the water's edge on squares of plywood on an outgoing tide.

These boys live[22] in the area of either side of the flag-marked safe beach and in the water beyond the little ones. Only rarely[23] do they approach the family clusters and they avoid[24] the girls of every age. When passage through the groups is unavoidable,[25] the flying sand in their wake sets off a paroxysm of grooming.[26] Inevitably, they leave their mark on their lotion-sticky elders. As evening approaches these boys will drift up the beach to watch the surfers, the adolescent males, absent from the afternoon beach scene.

It is midweek, the island has been scouted and this family beach is touched upon but seldom occupied by the far-ranging

[19] What ages, for how long, how related? Weak!

[20] See 18. The word *ignore* observer's? Or signal from children—remember British male signaling that he does not see female in hotel lounge.

[21] Get this on film for microanalysis. This may be important to making "territory" less sloppy. Look for nonadversary, nonownership behavior in "territory."

[22] Same as 21.

[23] "Rarely" implying "seldom"? Or is this only frequency statement? Can I find out what I think I mean here?

[24] Observer's term? Or signal? Need film, can't see. Theory impoverished.

[25] Same as 24.

[26] Same as 21.

teenage boys. When one makes an appearance, he moves with hurried purpose.[27] Searching out a particular group, he spends but a few moments and then heads back uncaptured. From time to time older boys come down the beach to stand in passing communion with the guards.[28] Their passage links station to station.[29] And while they take census, they swing toward the water to avoid[30] the untimely demand made by eddys of female activity. When one does approach the girl groups, he stands just at the edge of the group's area. He shifts from foot to foot for a short period and then departs, perhaps to wave, safe down the beach or as he takes sanctuary[31] upon the dune. There, only his momentary clumsiness, his passing loss of stride, gives evidence of his uncertainty, the mixed impulse to flight or involvement.[32]

Several pages of the journal are omitted here. Footnotes are numbered consecutively for reader's convenience.

When the sea is flat and the shore breeze brings the little black flies, the greenheads and mosquitoes, bathers and fishermen retreat in a common misery. And a chill, wet Northeaster empties sea and beach alike. But today the surf line marks two universes. Those beside and in the sea are contiguous but distant from those upon it.[33]

Few upon the beach register the making of the birds and

[27] Same as 24.

[28] Disinvent "groom"—as obscurationist as "agonistic" in social situation.

[29] Does "station" in structural analysis have same shortcoming as "role" in the study of groups?

[30] Review theory (data?) re: avoidance behavior. Still make sense?

[31] Why "sanctuary" and not "station"—data?

[32] Is this the name of the act—is this a signal about "inside" or observer's psychologistic loss of discipline—film. (Can't.) Watch!

[33] Do we have an idea that can help here? "Niche" is obviously a bad analogy. Are Whorf and Buckminster Fuller both right? Do we act in the planes we can talk about? Or is talk here no more than a sufficient reference medium?

the gathering of the fleet. Fewer still mark its break and spread.[34] Word passes among the boys that there are fish up the beach and this is sufficient. The guard reassures an elderly woman that there has been no drowning up the beach and this is sufficient. From the boats, the beach is as it should be. It has no events and the people there are but features of an irrelevant[35] landscape. On their first day at the shore, parents point out the boats near the beach (for only boatmen and fishermen see those far out). By midweek the bathers see no boats—their universe is beach bounded.

The change from city apparel to beach clothes prepares my eye for beach undress.[36] A quick survey as I cross the dune and skirt the emplacements is interspersed with double take and surreptitious peek. At times a glance has been satiating, the entrance to the beach scene, a limited performance. This is not a beach to be seen on; the observer need not reward display with stare. The lone observer makes easy entrance with no need to censor as when with a female companion, no need to look loudly as with a fellow male. Without demand to signal observation, the scene is for the viewing.

The first sharp sense of bodies, bodies everywhere fades, and shape, skin, fat, meat, bones, color, and texture lie displayed upon the sand. Shapes like skinny, lean, bony, and skeletal, particularly manifest in their rarity on this beach, give way before the solidity, the fleshiness, the ripeness, the fullness, the fat, and the obese. I must discipline my eyes to make them work for me. If I did not, in my happy mood, they would show me only pretty sights. And so I look again: Fat-rippled

[34] Is interview enough here—relationship between "register" and "recall"? "Mark" may be better.

[35] Psychological interpretation or sociological description?

[36] Is this the proper stage for participant observer—at the point of problem location rather than at that of investigation test?

Remainder of paragraph about investigator. Should be analyzed by outside investigator. Autobiographic technique can be illusory here. What is this and following about? Ventilation or report on micro–culture shock?

thighs lead the eye upward expectably to roll upon roll or to surprise as corpulence gives way at hipline to slender body. Bony legs may attach to bony body but at times they meet sudden bulge; protuberance on matchsticks.

Flesh can be firm, the bones in light disguise, muscles in tonus; the whole an unreliable testament to love and care and health. Or, and this, while unusual, makes its mark by its presence: a chair full of flesh, a constant reminder to all who can afford to view its shapelessness. A terrifying and revolting example, the woman inside is out of sight. But she is only by degree less visible than is the girl who studied Hollywood and grew to pattern. Each move she makes is a move of practiced prominences. There is no person there, just as there are no persons in the bunches of muscles that flex and parade connected by the toss of beachball, and by inattention to this girl or any other.

In my revolt I change my lens; new focus should provide relief. Goiter, acne, scar, and disproportion are dominant figures in the new field of vision. These fade and give way to bulbous nose, crooked teeth, peeling shoulders, and a range of stigmata from open sore to Band-Aid and bandage. I turn from adult and seek a younger field. There is no surcease there in the mongoloid puff, the twisted leg, the half-staggering gait, the emptied faces; a clumping of anomaly that seizes my attention and screens out the other children on the beach.

With their viewing though, all of these fade into field, hardly so much as background for the people on the beach . . . if there be people there at all. A self-conscious spectator, I reverberate in dismay at the meanness of my selectivity. In a millisecond survey of the beach, I had seized upon the anomalous, the inappropriate, the anachronistic, and the bizarre. Yet, the quick fade of all of these makes the invisibility of the stressful universe comprehensible. There are those upon the beach who move throughout the afternoon in loud pronouncement of their relationship to the offensive and pitiable deviancies. These, too, are erased and with their charges become transparent to be seen through or moved around like any other steady and irrelevant feature of the beach. I watched latecomers scan the population of the beach, register and avoid these abnormalities. Trivial to the bather's afternoon, the unusuals are normalized by categorical dismissal. For me this brought reassurance that mine were not sensations, hypersensitive and calloused, occasioned by ten years in a medical milieu. That decade had brought new words but no new shape[37] to my registration system.

Even more astonishing is that positive impression is transitory, too. The first sweet view of beauty, of soft curve or appealing bone shape, of silken skin or lovely hair, if it does not gain other relevance, is a passing thing. The reassurance of a beautiful childshape has little permanence, no more than manshape or womanshape. Once noted, these passed into the whole, often to be unrecoverable as point, but as influences in pattern. There was an elegant white-haired woman there, her posture serene and the skin on her face and hands old ivory. But she became a Beautiful Elderly Woman. The capitalization was indelible and although I tried I saw no more than that. Perhaps that's what her family brought to the beach.

My father, whom I had brought to the beach a few weeks before, had spent his days in delighted observation. His "there's every kind of people here" may have given rebellious focus to the scenes that impressed themselves upon the dissolving after-image of the bizarre.[38]

I look in vain for long, straight-combed, blond hair and for

[37] Irving Howe, who was good enough to read this, did not like the terms referring to "shape." I do because I think I'm dealing here with external appearance. "Appearance" is not anthropometric state. Rather it is a shared term. "Beauty" not only is not in the eyes of the beholder but it is not in that beheld—but *is* a statement of relationship. Beauty is not a binary reciprocal with ugly—beauty and ugliness as ritual? What is a proper no-beauty?

[38] Seeing trees vs. forest—a function of instructions to focus? A batesonian metacommunication? I.e., is *moral* perception a social adaptation for protection of groups? Figure and field, particle and wave, pattern and particular, act and scene—should not be confused with recent distortions of etic and emic.

tall, slim, trim bodies. The absence of Negroid feature, hair form, or color takes precedence over prevailing aspects of the landscape. The figures that dominate the field of view are negative, active by their absence, and they force the mind to map the larger stage. Sudden quiet can be extraordinarily loud. A break in pattern or expectancy, a real event that can demand review and explanation.[39] In postponement of this, or, perhaps, to check the reality of my strong impression, I catalogue my surround: Hair, jet black to brown, is matched by eyes. Most of the bodies are blocks and toward the sturdy side. The distance from knee to foot tends toward the short and forearms toward the muscular. Skin color is dark to pallid olive. And, although within the afternoon's span there are taller men and women on the beach, my almost six feet give me a reassuring sense of height, the rosy cast to my tan, a feeling of health and propriety.

This is a selected population. It differs from that of other beaches—just as they differ from one another. Yet, selection is a long-term word and I wonder what it means in this connection. In fantasy I am in the midst of a school of people drawn by imaginable instinct to their niche and uninvaded by competitive species. I and a few others are solitary migrants swimming through their territory. Such fancies titillate, but neither these nor my determination to restrict my attention to the beach itself are satisfying. They cannot preclude the set that two years of studying distributions on the Jersey shore has given. Why some groups are here and others not becomes a preoccupation. The here-now[40] I attempt to see in gains depth and breadth, and I need a map to give perspective to my viewing, to give me context and control so that I can see again in more than bits and pieces.

[39] Structural principle—absence is like the phone not ringing or the middle-class man without a wedding ring?

[40] Howe did not like this either. The here-now, there-then distinction is clumsy but the social shape of allopsychic orientation is stored in mutual behavior. Mutual? Do I mean shared? Probably not, since I'm not dealing with something inside people but with something integral to *social* regularity.

In search for that perspective I play the mind-film in reverse and follow my beachmates backward from the shore. Many, if not most, return to cars tagged *La Belle Province*. Their retreat takes them past signs that say "*Nous parlon Francais* . . . Welcome Canadians." They cross the bridge and recede up the parkway into New York and finally across the border to Montreal. Others from the beach do not go back north at the parkway, but roll west to the suburbs of Camden, to the lower-middle-class wards of South and West Philadelphia, on west to similar areas in Pittsburgh and its suburbs or north toward Scranton and beyond. Usually there is a Catholic church and school in the neighborhoods to which they return; the houses they return to are clean and neat and the area is called "respectable."

With the exception of a few from Montreal, it will be by accidental overlap that those from this beach meet each other back home. They are not friends but beach acquaintances and vague beach promises do not hold upon return.[41] They will meet next season without recrimination but with regrets that the work season kept them apart. They hold white-collar ambition, Catholicity, and vacation spot in common. The first two of these, shaped by past and hope for future, keep them separate back home, and mere propinquity does not force them together at the shore. This is a family beach, a multifamily beach, a *vacation* beach, and neither insular family nor vacation is adulterated by courtship, business, or obligation in either setting. Separate but adjacent at home, they are separate and adjacent at the shore.

Time slowly rolled backward in a single line can provide trajectory but perspective can be blurred by search for cause. Uniqueness is all too often a function of focus. At times the nature of a group is illuminated if not revealed by recognition

[41] "Friend"-"acquaintance." Is this a spatio-temporal distinction? What are rights and duties in a communicational sense? Think about spacing-out to permit intimacy or to protect against it. Is intimacy a statement of a closed (information-excluding) system or what?

of larger groups to which it does not belong and of still larger ones to which it does.[42]

The next section is included because it's *about* theory—I think.

We didn't learn much about gravity in the fourth grade from the teacher's tale of Pisa. That the Tower leaned was interesting, that objects dropped from it fell to the ground was unsurprising, that a small and large one hit the ground at the same time was further proof of Miss Geyer's gullibility or adult mendacity. At recess we concluded that Italians were tricky. (A few grades later, with absolutely no faith in its veracity, we were to impress younger ones with the information that a pound of feathers and a pound of lead would land together.) I was to be in college before this aspect of gravitational phenomena had more than myth or grade or status value. There was a period then when I believed it.

The salt-flour map we made did make sense, however. What goes up must come down and water always runs downhill. On the classroom globe it was downhill from north to south and while we never quite understood the Great Lakes and the St. Lawrence, the flow of the Ohio and the Missouri into the Mississippi and to the Gulf seemed reasonable. The Appalachians were high points, and that water flowed down their sides eastward to the Atlantic was sensible, that rills become rivulets to become creeks and finally rivers that dumped into the sea made sense, too. Years later on my first trip east, I had pleasure in a mountain rainstorm. In my imagination I raced the droplets to the sea.

The eastern slope is a vast drainage system that tips seasonally to slide its inhabitants to the sea. Thousands of cars surge eastward along the Pennsylvania Turnpike, other thousands come down the Northeast Extension. Some follow the Turnpike across the great bridge into New Jersey. Others flow through the Schuylkill Gap into Philadelphia, their stream fed

[42] Again, again—Pike needs reading and testing by a trained but uncommitted Ph.D. candidate.

by the tens of thousands of cars from Chestnut Hill, Germantown, the Main Line, and North Philadelphia. Other streams arise in the southern and western industrial section and become confluent to race to crest at the Delaware. From high above can be seen four flumes. The Benjamin Franklin, Walt Whitman, Tacony-Palmyra, and the Delaware Memorial bridges carry the shoreward flows, torrents that will feed one another but never merge in a single flood.

New Jersey is not tinted pink to contrast with Pennsylvania's green as on our salt-flour map, but there is solace for childish map recall as Pennsylvania's humus and rock give way at borderline to New Jersey's sand. Northern New Jersey is an inland area, but the beach that borders it broadens until it is statewide here. The car streams flow into this alluvial plain. They divide repeatedly as though through delta land to solve the passage to the sea and come to rest in a thousand settlement basins. The journey is at an end; the dunes have stopped the rolling cars. Gravity has had its way and the flow from inland height to dead sea level is complete.

The analogy is exhausted. I cannot imagine why drops of water that fall in Minnesota rush down the Mississippi together and then choose different bayous just before the journey's end . . . and people are at least as complicated as raindrops.

Analogy replaces analogy in the absence of new information: The eastern slope is a vast computer; the cars are cards to be spit out by program into shoreline resting slots. The cars are coded for final destination; their pathways a function of shuffle and sort. Many cards slide through on a single sort to give simple identity to the slot in which they come to rest. For these there were no alternatives. Other cards seem flipped by chance factor, by machine error or by whimsy to drop askew, their disarray a signal for re-sort. Made visible, some cling to place and by this action change the slot. Others rest awhile in nonfit, a temporary disturbance for they will be repunched. Another year may find them up or down the Jersey shore.

Shunted at an early gate, they can be punched for other channels: south to the Chesapeake or north to Cape Cod or to Maine. The error may not be in punch hole but in card shape, the sea a false destination. There is a simple alternative; they are reassigned by the mountain code. Or, this failing, programmed by auto club or by travel bureau, they slide across America or Europe, restless cards set to search through slots and then return.

This imagery gives substance to my statistics, a poetic analog, modern and fearsome, because it idealizes the machine and makes people holes in cards, their choices comprehensible because they did not have to make them—and because it allowed them to be random in a universe in which they were the only things that were.

They told me dogs were only animals and I used to wish I could take one apart to see what made it come when I called it, what made it run when I turned it loose. But the only dog around was mine and he and I both knew he was not just an animal so I took apart a wind-up toy. There was a little spring inside and gears that turned and worked the legs and then I understood. But then a truck opened up a dog down on the road and, no adults around, I looked inside the dog and found no springs and gears but still I understood. Toy dogs, their gears and wheels were for little boys, enough to know . . . and a protection for the secrets of little dogs. Later, I would understand substitute explanation and, generally, it would satisfy me.

The computer is dominated by program and selection, a function of machine. New Jersey is not a machine. Those that head toward the shore are not shuffled by whirling teeth that catch on cardpunch and are not by gear gated to destination. And the gates themselves are open. The signs that mark the choice points list no criteria, no shape to test the punch hole or its position. There are no computer operators to check credentials, to replace bent cards or, even, to repair jammed machine —and, in fact, on earth, no programmer. But perspective provided by analogy is perspective explanation. The discovery of the shape of nonfact and of the organization of ignorance reduces search. Our models have not been wasted for they permit us to see order and regulation. And yet, because they do not explain, they could, by twisted logic, become evidence that the order we perceive is happenstance; the movement of the whole an emergent accident, the accidental clumping of individual action, the pseudoorder of coincidence.

The model here is easy to construct: Take an organism and shape it by conditioning, by punishment and reward (direct or indirect), and turn it loose and it will run obediently to the sea. Or, if the Condition is too hard to conceive, his master plan too intricate to build from tiny pieces, then the organism can be supplied with "mind" and "will," and action made explicable as thrust from internal engine with control and direction a function of choice. But this is mischievous, semantic play. There is no conditioner, no master plan, and no conditioned organism. Other people's poetry should not be literalized, their analogies made real to tease them with. Conditioning as conditioning, like gravity, is an omnipresent process, and, as such, no explanation. Neural arcs and networks are conditioned, there are no people there. And it is unfair to take a model designed to dispense with "instinct," "mind," and "will" and test it out with human beings. That's not what it's about. Organisms are systems in which neural networks are always traceable but organisms are not made from neural networks. Human beings are systems in which organisms are always present but human beings are not simply organisms. The distance from neural arc to human being is a journey of several universes, with times and spaces that cannot be transcended in a single leap.

I talked with the boys from Rutgers, biologists who told me of the birds that swept the shore. The Latin names they gave the gulls and terns dignified their talk and I was impressed as they spoke of territories and special niche division. They told me why they thought each group was where it was and I was satisfied. They knew how sparse my knowledge was. I made their general statements facts and they became polite. My title and gray hair claimed respect but I closed issues wiser men kept open and etiquette replaced the give and take of peers. To regain fellowship I traded talk. I told them of the French-Canadians, of the hyphenated Americans who rested on my beach. That second-generation Italian and Sicilian, Pennsylvania Dutch, and German-Irish mixes predominated here gained me their ears. And, since they had their beaches, too, they listened when I talked about beach selection—the distribution of populations along the shore. "Why?" they asked and were too soon content with the reply, "It's a matter of communication." They understood when I did not, made facts of my hypotheses, patronized me, and left me alone to people watch.

Some material is skipped here.

The shape of beach and span of vacation time are dimensions of the organization we perceive.[43] There are many beaches and Americans can, according to their wants, find novelty or familiarity.[44] They may even *seek* one or the other if they are sufficiently aware to recognize either when they find it. They could go to resorts that guarantee to laminate by age and segregate by gender, where family doings are matters of passing reassurances. Or, as on our beach, where only adolescent boys are freed from family tie, the family is bound together for a week: To separate to make connections would diffuse control. They save to go to better beaches and they are proud that they are not on those where riff-raff go.[45]

[43] "Perceive" is too psychological. We need terms for what in technical terminology is called an "ethnographic present." "Perceive" here is an observer's term. We need three terms: one for analyst, one for participant, and a third for the shifting field.

[44] "Novelty" and "familiarity" have always been difficult for me. I don't even know how to think about the contrast much less study it (or them).

[45] Test.

They save not for their own, but for their children's sakes; most return each year until the children "go away," the beach, except in memory, a generation long. Some will buy to stay upon the island when they retire. They rent the second floor to save a place to which their children and the children of their children should return. There are those families for which this works and there is an enviable continuity to their lives. For these few, generation overlaps with generation; the old folks make friends who trade familiar talk; stability without tradition[46] is characteristic of their lives.

Our beach has a few who come down for the day, the Saturday or Sunday bathers, who help populate the sand but who move in between the occupants of the beach. They pack a week into a day. The frenetic pace of their activity is masked by the uneasiness of those who plan to stay the week but have not yet found a tempo consonant with the time they have to spend. There are the families who have the weekend, who pack as though to stay a week and when unpacked must repack to get away: the trip to the beach a problem in logistics. And, yet, those weekenders leave their mark upon the beach: Their harried departure is satisfaction for those who do not have to leave, the frantic angry scramble a lesson overlearned by those who have six days to go. By Monday the weeklies have settled in upon the shore. Aware that time has passed, they must press to rest before the week is done. For most this will be a hurried rest; by Thursday they will begin to start to leave, in part from faith that slower pace will soften termination.

Clocks and calendars are handy things to make divergent pathways intersect, to avoid collision and, by overstructure, to permit variation and internal change. Stores upon the island close by clock and so do restaurants; preachers preach by

[46] Should study this. Probably won't. Students so enamored of a cheapened version of systems theory that "stability" gets confused with "homeostasis." "Tradition" requires a student who knows what folklore is not about as well as understanding some of the things it's used for.

clock, policemen measure speed, and beachboys open and close the beach by clock. The children watch the clock to catch their favorite programs and father stays alerted for fear he'll miss the game and mother times the meals lest appetite turn into hunger and, yet, they speak of the timelessness of the midweek, the plateau between arrival and departure that marks Vacation.[47]

On Thursday, calendar joins clock in shaping time. Father checks the time remaining with the money he has left and mother checks the clothes; money-time and clothes-time are very real when placed in context. I wonder why relativity was not more evident to those who needed concepts of time with which to measure things. Nor are the children heedless to the changing shape of hours and days. On the first days of the week, hours and days have room within for pleasure, but they accelerate and squeeze as midweek passes. Parental cues or internal clocks signal the approaching end to vacation time and the children act to stay the terminating action. Denial that time has passed, when disproved, gives way to hint or plea or demand that time should be extended, that departure be postponed.

I watched and listened week after week, but could not tell if children started delaying action on their own or merely followed family regulation. I could not determine whether the signaled wish to extend beach time was more than an expression of the child's role in the family drama. It often seemed as though the children's reluctance to leave was but an obedient response to parents who had set the time aside for them. The parents knew but I did not, an important issue if blame or credit is at stake.

[47] How do you study "time?" Interviews are things we do with words to get material stored in words. I guess I'll study space and time arrangements all my life. Maybe that is what underlies all of structuralists' gobbledygook. Tense is confusing but perhaps only because it is a lexical, syntactical-lexical concept. Find the shape! Neither space nor time are directly observable apart from the behavior they are. Thus only conceivable.

Part of the journal is omitted here.

It is difficult to stop a stream of events in time and not be persuaded that the earlier events not only precede the later ones but cause them. Only when we recognize the stream as a single event, a structure in which sequence and priority are not relevant to cause, can we proceed in our analysis. On Thursday, parents begin to prepare to leave and children begin to drag their feet, an occasion for family negotiation. Ritualistic and real, the interchange is an extended incident, an orderly procedure, unpredictable to its performers.[48]

For all their differences there are common lifeways among the beach folk: On Thursday the shore becomes a playing field, a game begins that lasts two days. In all the families I observed, the *shape* of family politics appeared the same. (White pawn advances and black responds; the choice of white, conventional.) The children let the parents know, then work on mother. Her vote or, at least, her nonopposition secured, they petition father and then help him impose his will, or lack of it, on mother. By Friday night the die is cast: They'll go or stay, a matter of decision, or, the decision delayed too long, they'll go and play the game again next year, shaped, but seldom educated, by this year's encounter.

Each child has a special repertoire, a particular style, a unique cast to his or her performance; identity and personality (as well as temperament) contribute to the way he or she makes a bid or engages in response. Parents are individual people, too. But, even when insane, their activities with others are a variation on a theme. This is a theme that is ultimately comprehensible—unless it is hidden in a mystique of individualism, buried in imposed categories, or forgotten when it does not submit to easy enumeration.

A generalization cannot cover every case and it is difficult, from my data and from my vantage point, to be sure but it

[48] This is a strange sentence. Make up your mind, Ray. Are you going to make ritual less than real—sticks and stones!

seems to me that ethnic patterns have given shape to the petitions and responses I observe. The pouty, mouth-twisted whine of the French-Canadian child systematically differs from the sullen, dark-browed quiet of the child from the Pennsylvania Dutch country—who is more mute but no less messageful. And there is no confusing either of these with the Italian-American child, who moves from mood statement to mood statement with almost no markers of transition. His demanding clamor or soft-spoken inducements are audible accompaniments of tears that course down a smiling face giving way to puckishness, somehow a combination of grief and delight or, more likely, a wry comment on both of these. And the styles of these children will not be confused with the announced partial commitment of the Irish-American child, whose open choir-face, wide-eyed and sweet, gives way upon frustration to compressed lips and angry glare and these, upon detection, to cajoling smile and corner-wrinkled eyes.

I find predictability, too, in the way the game is played out. There is no implication here that national origin is an irresistible force that operates down through the generations to determine action; but tested observation deserves report. The Pennsylvania Dutch, regardless of the attractions of the shore, seem to stay out their plan and depart on time, the budget sacred as with the French-Canadians, who, however, often stay two weeks, the first of which is trial to test out worth before they settle for the real week. The Italian-Americans tend to stay an added week, sometimes two—the money can be found somehow. In fact, all, including me, were surprised and somehow disapproving, when an Italian-American father called his office to extend his stay and, when refused, quit the job and seemed undaunted about his next. But the Irish-Americans seemed most complex in game-play and negotiation. Whim and mood seemed to dominate decision. And yet there is order too in the regularity of promise quickly given and then denied, of justified refusal and unexplained acquiescence, the press of uncertainty, regular and regulated—the consistency of the certainty that any decision, once made, is somehow wrong.[49]

In the quiet of early Friday morning, tethered dogs, a little fat and combed, were walked by owners who met upon the walk and pulled against the dogs, who, out of territory, had problems of identity and would rather sniff than kiss or fight, a matter of embarrassment for the owners, who thought the dogs had communication wrong end to. There were no children out. Only in the evening do they enjoy the space between the cottages and the beach, a territory alien and empty, except as carry-over from beach play. The gulls around are quiet. Most are off to the garbage dump or, the tide right, to feed undisturbed upon the beach. The remaining few seem uncommunicative and they sit quietly upon the poles or search scraps of paper without much interest; they seem a little tired this morning, like the man across the way who gathers bottles tossed out of cars the night before.

From the phone booth across the street a woman heads back toward her apartment, eyes fixed straight ahead. No car can hit her if she does not look and, besides, her children are all married and she is somehow invulnerable. She ignores the angry screech of brakes, unnecessarily applied. She does not speak to strangers and her pursed lips are sufficient reply to male exasperation. Militant and monolithic, her gait somewhere between trudge and waddle, on the walk she is not as heedless as she appeared in the road. Her eyes swiftly scan the windows and she pauses in half-stride as edgy-voiced family talk invades the quiet and occupies the space that will not be there when the complex is awake. She smiles the only smile I saw her make that morning, a quick twist of mouth with thrust of chin and lateral droop of lips, a smile because of eye involvement, a small and transient bit, given meaning by the

[49] All or any part of this must face the test of both situational and long-range data. What size, duration, focus is needed to test these statements? What size piece from one is comparable to what size from another? Can an investigatory film be made of each of these?

untouching hands that meet and rest in complacency below her sagging bosom upon her still-uncorseted abdomen. Her eyes narrow as she listens and her tongue comes out, its bottom caressing her protruding lower lip. I could not help but feel that she thought nature was in its proper place.

And then this woman, whom I could hardly bear to watch, by change of pace took me by surprise. A door had opened and from the end apartment came a younger woman, laden with dirty clothes that overfilled a plastic basket. The lightness of her step and the half-skip she used as she stepped down to the walk were matched by her grace of carriage and openness of face. Not a pretty woman, the texture of her skin too coarse, and while not fat, her face seemed to me as I had watched her the day before, to be at the edge of sag. Her hair stood up in overcomb, the coarseness of its texture magnified by mucilage. The roots still blond: She'd had it done a week before, an announcement that she did not intend to get into the water. And yet, her open-lidded, clear-eyed sweep of the morning, and the softness of her mouth and the tone to her face and form made me look again and this time as a male with some appreciation. Perhaps to increase my pleasure at the younger woman, I glanced for contrast at the older one. And then came the surprise: The weary, complaining walk that had so bothered me gave way to stride and with subtle and exquisite changes of pace she timed her movement with such precision that she and the younger woman met before the car.

"Oh," the older woman said, her tone raising just to fall again, like her mouth, which remained open, a signal of surprise and greeting and, even, readiness for social interchange. Her eyes abandoned slit and opened to fix upon the clothes, which the younger woman tried to cover even as she put them inside the car. The older woman stood alert, in projected quiet, only the drooping at the corners of her open mouth, the hands across her stomach maintaining former pose.

"Hi," the young woman said as though the only message she'd received was salutation. She stood, in smiling attention upon the older woman, but one foot moved as though it wished to leave her and get into the car. And even as she smiled she glanced away as though refusing to be fixed by the older woman's dominance. The customary lines between her brows deepened for an instant and, as the fingers of her left hand tightened on the handle of the car, her right arm rose to form a barrier: her biceps pressing along her breast, the lower arm upright between her breasts. For a moment in my imagination her in-turned, half-curled hand became a bird, transfixed and as if by nonmovement to signal that it was not or, perhaps, that it was all there was. The hand was to stay in that position, the forefinger curled and not quite touching her lower lip, until, moments later, safe inside the car, she had to turn the key to drive away. It seemed to me that both women moved around their hands, the fixed position of the older woman's hands above her stomach and the younger woman's arrested in the air a part of earlier streams of conversation, of messages continuing and incomplete, perhaps, only to be completed if the two became different people to themselves and to one another.

Two seconds elapsed during "Oh" and "Hi," and the older woman talked again as soon as "Hi" had reached her ears. "I see [her eyes upon the clothes] that you've managed so you can stay another week." Her shape of smile had teeth, and the narrowing of her eyes, the flatness of her voice, the overhigh and overloud emphasis on "managed" an accusation that widened the younger woman's eyes for just an instant. And then, her head cocked and eyes alight and with a smile (her lips a little thin but then they were seldom filled), the younger said, "Yes, my husband called his office. . . ."

The sentence was incomplete (no pitch change over "office") but it was not allowed to hang there long. The older woman, her face in sag, her shoulders drooping one bit more, in those moments put on weight and said, not in reply but in continuation of a conversation of her own, "We plan to buy some day." The tone was flat, the emphasis on "plan," a point of pitch and loudness and touched by drawl.

The left hand of the younger woman released the car and moved as though it would touch the older woman and without pause retook the door handle. As it did, the cloud that crossed her face was gone and in mock gay the woman laughed, a thin-pitched sound that stuttered through her nose before it sank into her throat and she got into the car. "Well," she said, and voice and body and change of position were messages of encouragement, regret, and salutation. And that was all the sound there was until her engine took hold and ground a little as she drove away. The older woman stood more erect and with her left hand swept imaginary crumbs off her dress while her right flipped backhand downward across her hips. Her eyes were not in focus on any object I could see and she went around the corner to her door.[50]

Gregory Bateson used to wonder how the individual feathers on a bird got the signal to be black or white to enable them to play their role within the patterns of that species' coloration. We talked about the learning of a gene pool and at first I thought he talked in metaphors. I could not conceive because of my restricted sense of nature that a gene pool had the qualities of a thing, a whole that changed through time. My perceptions of space and time were limited by preconception, and I thought him careless or poetic when he insisted that the pool was real, could test and store, discard and retrieve within the realities of its own spatio-temporal universe.

We often talked until late at night about whether pattern or particle came first in the storage of a master plan that could be revealed in genotypic resemblances. It was clear that neither chicken nor egg came first but plan for both chicken and egg,

[50] I cannot conceive of the devices necessary to make an investigatory film with sound of *a* person. A didactic one, yes, even a two-person picture would probably have to be hours in duration and even then could not be analyzed except as history. It takes at least three to communicate, or at least I don't know how to study ones and twos in terms of communicational theory. See astronomy—two-body problem.

delivered by egg and tested in the limited surround of groups of chickens. Like Bateson, I had been trying to make sense of human communication, and as over the years we talked I realized that his approach through time made sense of certain things I saw within my limited synchronic laboratory. And there was no surprise when DNA and RNA filled in conjecture with some mechanics of signal storage and delivery. Some of my friends still seem to think that this is what words are all about.

However, while from these conversations emerged a model for searching for the answers to problems of continuity in nature, from the beginning I was restless with a theoretical position that made words the only place humanity had to store its knowledge, the sole vehicle of social change and continuity. It seemed to me that the complexities of social organization, that the demonstrable malleability of humanity, its adaptive skill and the determined conservation of its adjustments could not be understood if all we looked at were words or the remnants of those words in writing or in artifact.

Bateson and I have long been agreed that, while particle provides the possibility of immediate variation, pattern precedes particles. Furthermore, we agree that pattern, looked at through time or in structured lamination of the here-now, is itself, from another view, a particle that gains its operative stability and resilience through its own position as aspect of overpattern. With Scheflen, we worked out a scheme by means of which each pattern could be seen as context for the particles it contained. Theoretical life became easier for me when I learned, by observational research, that system after system gains flexibility because particular particles are not limited to specific patterns. It is now possible to hypothecate within a scheme we may some day comprehend that each particle is a piece of behavior and that, if the system is not to become too rigid, too limited in function to permit change, this behavior must itself operate in many patterns. Perhaps this is one of the things it's all about: An increase in structure brings an increase in adaptability.[51] The controls supplied by structure make variability possible. And, variability within pattern is the nature of viable structure.[52]

[51] Interesting—but without a way of dealing with the concept of complexity this remains a poetic statement—easy to do with *a priori* classes. We lack data.

[52] This is probably the reason that talk about sign versus symbol in communication bores me.

For My Father

❂ ❂

EDWIN SCHLOSSBERG

Edwin Schlossberg is the author of *Wordswordswords*, *Einstein and Beckett*, and coauthor of *Projex*, *The Pocket Calculator Game Book*, *The 1977–1978 CB Guide*, and *The Philosopher's Game*. Dr. Schlossberg lives in Chester, Massachusetts.

Dear Gregory Bateson and subsequent readers,

I am writing to you but more accurately with you in mind. I have been having a conversation with you as I proceeded through your written works and the following words have precipitated out as an evidence of this conversation. The writing has no dramatic order since I think, as you do, that progress toward a climax is destructive of discovery and homeostatic organizations of thought.

The idea of a society being climax oriented rather than being organized around nonprogressive change immediately comes to light in the way an essay is written. If the essay sets up a climax by withholding information from the reader at the start and then slowly builds to the essence of the thinking, then the essay supports climax organization. That is not to say that there can be no plan in the structure of an idea to make it clearly understood but only that the process of structuring it and designing the experience can be done with the idea of progressively changing the thinking without coming to some dramatic moment when everything is revealed in the course of a few sentences.

It is interesting that often the subject or content of an idea is contemplated carefully but the context for its presentation is simply drawn from the tradition of written contexts. I felt that if I did that I would be continuing in the tradition of unconscious acts of exclusion and so this letter proceeds. Seeing the form reveal itself encourages the directness of the content.

We have all read texts where the words become challenges to the thinking of the reader and then the reader responds with critical indignation and writes another book and so on (reminiscent of Swift's *Battle of the Books*). So we progress through generations of criticism without a moment of contemplation of the context of the discussion and whether or not the thoughts bear any relationship to the act of their being read and understood. We thus find ideas and areas of thought barren of actual feelings and appropriate responses destroyed by a schismogenesis of thought brought about because of the reluctance to accept nonprogressive dynamic change and because of the reluctance to include the content of the idea's communication as part of the experience and, therefore, as part of the ideas.

Certainly we must assume that the place and means by which we read is supremely influential in how and what is the result of reading. The relationship between author and reader is an example of the way the social matrix is constructed and if this is not direct then no matter what the ideas are, they will be perceived as commands, not discussions, as trying bits of authoritarian behavior rather than the desire to create with integrity an experience that may perhaps provide an insight into another individual's context formation.

If I decided to write about detailed sets of logic which you have created then my relationship to them would be obscured since I would be able to describe them without including the context of their emergence. It seems clear that if I wrote to you *about* something I would not be writing to you but for you and therefore creating an object rather than trying to realize a context where ideas could be experienced. Also, I would be engaging in the peculiar emotional role of asking you to read something not as a direct communication, but as a finished piece, of which you could only be a passive observer.

I am not interested in passivity at all and so the process of composing for me is an active process to relate through the context of these words how I think and therefore how I am thinking. The context and the content are interacting and making me as present as I can be without the alienating posture of describing an objective reality—whatever that might be.

Finding that the beginnings of sentences require the word *I* to be placed there for legitimacy suggests that we encourage the generation of a calculus of selves heralded by the fictitious *I*, which ironically sounds too much like an organ of sight when in fact it appears as an evidence of blindness. The need to be present in words is remedied by the epigrammatic stating of referencing metaphors. In this way I am relived rather than relieved. The need to accept the organization of experience and context as an *I* and then the rejection of that organization as the sign for it (since it is not a fixed indicator but dynamic and nonprogressing) suggests the location of one of the sources of terror of the double bind syndrome. In order to accept another person's importance one must accept one's own importance and also one's own frailty. Something that does not exist cannot be threatened. However, the longer a person is willing to subvert his understanding of self, the longer that subversion requires its own codification. The words of a sentence can describe their own confusion but only in order. Perhaps what we are witnessing here is the emergence of evidence of the progressing complexity that any interactive experience entails and requires. In order for a double bind to exist it must evolve. In order to reveal the laws of this sentence one must look outside of the words within it.

The importance of presenting an adequate and dynamic context reveals itself in the manner in which a description takes form. If the words are not well chosen, if the syntax is not well organized, if the means of the viewing of the letters is not obvious, then the possibility of constructing a complement with the existing context is made difficult. In writing to you it is necessary for me to be one of the viewers of the process so that I can become both sender and receiver and thus neither, and we can all experience the processing of the context rather than simply me doing my work in my corner.

And you have to spell well because otherwise the ambiguity of the message is verging on a set which, although potentially interesting, does not contain the self of expression. Who says something is as important as what is said, and to whom and where and when is almost as important as what is said. Loose organization of a context is essential as paralleled by a very well thought out complement. How can we read something in disorder? We read it as the expression of a comparison with order and can never get to the development of the expression of context. John Donne's "Anniversary" poems come to mind—expression about the loss of coherence in perfect and entrancing iambic pentameter. Context shift created by the tension of form and subject of discourse. The eyes have it.

In looking at the way the letters are formed or how the sentences get put together I become attracted by how much can be said through the distraction from the usual. Like the idea of habit being a source of efficiency. So the idea of skill and its actuality is an example of the efficiency of habit since the expression of this thought would be impossible if it were not immediately recognizable and then after consideration differentiated.

You mention that consciousness is always less than its context. It seems to occur so often that we propose an ever enlarged task for those processes in which we are interested. We become conscious and then ask for everything to become conscious thus reducing the experience to oblivion. If the words that were written could only embrace the truth of everything they would, in any specific case, be more liable to ineffective communication since the exact circumstances would not be appropriate. It would be like rehearsing a thought and not realizing that what you were doing was learning to exclude aspects of the communication rather than to include them. No context can be fully understood unless one is outside it and being outside of consciousness is filled with Wittgenstein's silence and our own.

Niels Bohr asks what we are talking about when we mention global issues since we have nothing with which to compare them and so they are meaningless. I think that what he was attending to was the idea of observation requiring exclusion of the observer on one level and then inclusion of the effects of that observation on another. But the shift in levels of observed aggregation was not attended to and so there was a little confusion. We say, "Be conscious," and I wonder who is talking and who is listening.

I read *Steps to an Ecology of Mind, Naven,* and *Our Own Metaphor,* and some articles that you wrote, and became aware of how much writing allows for evolution in the context of thinking. As you suggest, what evolves is the context and not the entities. To separate into context and then content would be like looking at the words in their etymological patterns rather than as the evidence of the process of thinking. This letter evolves because of its relationship to the writer, to the reader/writer, and so on, and not in and of itself. Perhaps if I rewrite it some day it will change, but it will be rewritten because the context in which it exists has changed and so requires alteration. It is interesting to me to think that your idea of context itself is an evidence of the evolution of context and that previous to now we thought to collect evidence in order to demonstrate the impossibility of explaining evolution with those things. Certainly the idea of classification becomes simply a storage mechanism rather than a mode of understanding. Nothing that we learn or utilize can be in the form of storage. An unopened book is storage. This sentence is storage except for now.

You discussed digital and analogic thought and the discussion was analogic, and I thought that perhaps what we learn about systems of logic is always retrospective and context creating. Describing the words on the page while writing them becomes only a progressively regressive act that requires the use of both analogy and digitalized methods of observation and organization. Every letter is chosen from all the possible letters but that choice, out of habit, is not actually made in a digitalized fashion. One learns to identify entire patterns and so the choice of words becomes digital but the work inside the word-analogic, and this suggests that these two aspects are always present. I write a sentence and that becomes a progressive revelation of earlier formulations and yet something entirely unto itself only as far as an analogy can be realized. What your eyes are doing is not the same as what my fingers, as I press the keys, are doing, except insofar as one extends each action as a part of a cognitive act and then, being so undifferentiated, we cease to be able to speak. Lately as I listen to music I realize how much our training is toward digitalized incorporation and the music that is becoming very interesting has to do with continuous tones. Again the context overrides the interest in the contents and we are of an environment and not in it. The *you* in letters becoming the *you* in mind. Yet each letter is separate, and each word, and each . . .

To sit and write allows for the interesting conversation to arise between a reader and the author if the author assumes the role of someone and not the transmitter of fact. In commenting on the process of realizing the text, the text becomes like a face on which can be perceived the messages concerning the reader. Every text is about its author but rarely is the text made to become as an author in the dynamic of reading. In the wish to communicate is the wish to be present and therefore part of the context through which learning proceeds. Exclusion of the awareness of the reader directs attention to the abstracted world of fact. There are these two so-called types of writing called fiction—therefore not about real life—and nonfiction—not not real. Obviously all is fiction until the moment of translation into experience and that effort involves the reader and writer jointly. Hiding in words is the ability to obscure the author and become the words. This set of words is an attempt to avoid that process and provide evidence of how to proceed to write and read within the context of words. No mind/body split even in the structuring of the text.

This becomes an attempt to conserve complexity of communication at the level of the context, syntax, and content. All parts contributing to the ambiguity and therefore the possible levels of meaning. Writing that this context contributes to the ambiguity in a clear expository sentence enhances the reader's understanding that my effort is not to confuse by reifying the words but to sustain the actual complexity of communication by getting involved in it as it.

You speak about complementary relationships where A responds to T's weakness, or competitive relationships where A responds to S's strength. For me to carefully work over your thoughts, my satisfaction or dissatisfaction with them would be to engage in those two paradigms. But to provide the evidence of how those thoughts have been integrated and processed in my mind through these words, I am trying to proceed nonprogressively and dynamically in my thinking. I measure my understanding by my ability to realize ideas through expression that contextually supports the thinking and describes it in content. Irwin Edman said (I am paraphrasing) that there were two types of people, those who divided the world into two and those who didn't. Then there are those who are writing reading and division resembles the white between the letters. If this text was printed on transparent paper my thinking would be that much more effective. If this text was printed on a mirror surface your thoughts perhaps could join more closely with mine. My poetry is written on clear surfaces and on mirrors and this text has to suffer the separation of opacity. Reflection is essential to be placed next to vision. Reflection vision.

I am aware that you will read these words one after another. That you read them transposes them into another context but one that I am trying to accommodate through discussion of the implications that writing has for reading. I am thinking about something very different now that you are reading this and the time break results in your creation of a context at least prepared for but not restricted. Moving your eyes over these marks on the paper is the physical act you are performing and that performance changes the experience entirely. By observing we create what we are looking at since the nervous system, as

Maturana so brilliantly describes, exists only in the present. The creation of an experience is the context of its unfolding and by progressively changing the location of intention we progressively shift that observation and therefore the observer. Over there in the field by the trees near the wind is the temperature I have been feeling. You were there while here and the suggestion of transposition should have affected more than simply your body heat.

In the formation of a thought there is such a wide range of possible methods by which to express that thought. Selecting that method which indicates the selective process and which suggests some of the exclusions makes the method selected the most attractive and compelling. When a sentence is read it is not the rules of reading or grammar formation that are attended to but the transformation of those rules by the content and structure of the text. Making the content and structure assume dynamic roles in the thinking, and therefore the design of the thought, allows for the code to be broken only insofar as the reader is willing to pay attention to how the words are coming and not only to what they "say." For instance the word no lies after word which compels attention to every level of its composition. It is a metacommunication in with the content communication and therefore throwing the whole process into consideration. How often we read about dynamic ordering of experience in the context of the dullest perceptions of language and syntax and structure.

Meaning comes through comparison. Sometimes the comparing exists within the verbal structure and sometimes within the analogies made with the given expression. By creating comparison we reduce the number of variables in a given expression and thereby increase the redundancy, the habit of thought. In order that we (the royal *we*) may *re*cognize it, we require two encounters and this realization requires yet another. It is so interesting that we must always include the variable of observation as yet another vantage point from which the present unrolls. Making a generalization about meaning and communication creates a meaning of meaning about meaning, which inevitably suggests yet another level of meaning. This is not regressive analysis but progressive. And as before, we must see it not as an increase but simply as a new state. This makes me think of your interest in the tribes which separated off and kept the same ritual formulations rather than start entirely new rituals as other tribes did. The groups that created entirely new social forms and rituals had to constantly compare themselves to their former selves. "Entirely new" was only in relation to the former social order. Therefore by creating an entirely new social order in reaction to the old they were more directly preserving the boundaries of the old than the group that would splinter off and reproduce, since the splinter group could vary ever so slightly without any recognition or comparison. The group that changed completely had to remember the old constantly in order to produce the new. Preservation does not always come in identical packages. Feedback must not only remind one of the message to act on but also to act against.

We all like to verify the appropriateness of our perception of our relationship to others. This can be done in so many ways. If I tell you how to do it that expresses a sense of perception of your relationship to me. If I proceed to describe my projected relationship to you through my words then you may not be able to respond as you would want to respond. If I express my concerns, my structuring the text so that as you read it it unfolds my understanding of your participation and contemplation, this seems most supportive and encouraging. I think of the beginning of one of Samuel Beckett's stories in which he says that he has already died. First line of the story. Well then, who wrote the text? Obviously the author could not have since he is already dead, except he did. The message is to pay attention to the communication and not strictly to the facts. The facts are written in fiction. Therefore, welcome to the present. The present is always at the end of a thought about the present.

The idea of writing in response to your ideas, Gregory Bateson, is very attractive to me since it allows me to function in a complementary way to the thoughts rather than trying to become them or to believe them. The shark, as you point out, has not learned about hydrodynamics but his body form is the solution of a hydrodynamic complement. Two aspects, the phenomenon under observation and the thinking about it, form the context. We usually look at one or the other and not the two as one. Looking at them separately was a function of the nineteenth-century need to collect and identify. Now we seek to observe and integrate and there are no edges, only varying methods of description. However, it should be noted that the variation in concern indicates a variation in intention. Formerly we were looking in order to identify and organize what was present in an environment. Now, as we have identified, we seek to learn why and how. It is as if we laid out a telephone service first and then had to learn what to say. We are laying out a two-way cable television service now and the efforts to integrate and understand the self/environment are a reflection of the demands that this type of participatory operation necessitates. We must stress the need for context observation and integration because it is needed, not because it is better or worse per se. No method of thinking can be considered an improvement outside of the context in which it arises. Where the environment was not disturbed by the activities of human beings and where it provided an integrated context for the species that lived there, comprehensive integrated approaches were not considered; no complementary forces existed. At the present, the environment and human beings are interaffecting to a great extent and so our thinking must reflect and participate in interactive, integrative formulas. The context has evolved and not our thinking alone. To think this way seems to realize much more of the process that is occurring and seems to necessitate the use of self/environment as the designation of what is being observed—or more importantly to the redundancy of the message—the how of observing.

What seems to precipitate out again and again is the thinking that change requires advance toward rather than expansion of or alteration with. If a concern that we have is important its presence in our thinking should not only be contained in the words chosen but witessed in the design and presentation of those words. Entropy seems a peculiar measure of the direction of so complex a context as human experience. Perhaps the changing awareness of complexity and the conservation of it, including the thinking about variation and observation, brings a more nearly useful approximation of what and how our concerns are. Yet there occurs the thinking that bringing to rational discourse the nature of our description requires that the all-embracing case of existence must now invent a slightly larger context out of which to operate. Just as human communication must invent new metastructures when previously useful but recently described metastructures become revealed (like body language), so perhaps we always open the mind to change through ever altering the nature of the way we describe and observe. This, however, goes out from this text and texts about thinking as writing, and so I will reserve it for a later message. (However, it is interesting to be able to talk about "later" in words since when they are actually communication it may already be later and my thinking would have been expressed. So "later" in words means a whole range of contexts when considered as such.)

We could say, and therefore have, that our relationship to the environment remains an idea as long as we neglect our presence in and of it. We worked to conquer nature in terms of physical intervention and now work to obliterate the boundaries so that we can enlarge our concept of self and our concept of environment so that any intervention is a disturbance to the context. In this way we continue to learn about ourselves by learning to understand the arbitrary nature of the boundaries. A young child absorbs our understanding by what physical and emotional messages are presented. If there were no toys, everything we presented would be considered as part of the environment rather than as models of it, and the relationships with others and within self would be witness to the connectedness and integration of perception/cognition. The young child with toys can only learn that things can intercede between self and environment and thus make short arcs of a circuit that is self/environment. Certainly words are some of the things we have used. Making objective reality exist between the person speaking and the person listening is an example of the creation of toys. We know that the person listening is creating from the words something that the person speaking could not have imagined. And making this part of the context of communication extends and gives importance to this realization. As I write you read, you read. . . . This being not a special case of the interaction but simply a *re*mind.

Often when writing, we accede to the notion that the conscious and explicit nature of thought is what it, the whole, is about. We talk with the assurance that bringing into conversation all aspects of a thought will in fact make the whole become more real and comprehensible. You mention Freud and I think about the serious practitioners looking in vain for the ego. Conscious representations are an aspect of the picture which is possible in conscious representations. Bringing every feeling, thought, and experience into words does not make the whole more comprehensible. In fact the paradoxes may increase at such an alarming rate that the possibility of behaving at all calmly may be impossible. That does not extend in powers, so-called, of the mysterious and unspeakable. It only gives the mind the range of limitations as to conscious verbal representations. Einstein said (I am paraphrasing) that the most incomprehensible aspect of the universe was that it was at all comprehensible. Bringing description into the range of precise analogies at all is part of the picture, an ever increasing and more interesting part, but only part. Trying to think of how my heart is beating would not be a replacement for its beating and control mechanisms as such. Exploration of the verbal description must have accepted changing boundaries. For example, the question "Who am I?" heads off into that seductive but impossible realm of thinking that has no use or function or delight.

I think of Wallace Stevens's poem "Man on the Dump."

Stevens describes how it feels to look for garbage in the one place where you can't find it—on the dump. On the dump it is all garbage and so there are no comparatives and trash means nothing. So the irony is that one goes to the dump to look for trash only to find that there there is no trash. One looks to the language and consciousness for the explanation of language and consciousness only to find that there there is no language and there is no consciousness. One writes a letter about thoughts only to find that thinking comes in the experience of the black lines on the white and not in them themselves. Paying attention in this way allows words and thinking to survive in the dynamic realm of continuing existence and processing. The final revelation is only the last one.

The skill of writing is to provide a context in which other people can think. Just as in any activity, the degree of its usefulness is whether or not it provides a context of communication. Talking about ecology as a separable and abstracted idea that has systems and cycles only catalogs the absence of an ecology. What we describe when we define is not the presence of something but the absence of it. When we say that the observer effects the observed, we have removed the dynamic and replaced it with two reified and unusable things that are supposed to be there. Am I an observer or the observed? Am I a context for experience or the receiver of the communication about what has been communicated? Are these words comprehensible or am I thinking about something which, by following these words in order, I can experience? When I read this is it a word or is it a referent to the processing that is occurring? Any answers are contained behind your eyes or not at all.

It is difficult to describe in words the problems that words have. It always points, this situation, to Wittgenstein's area that must be passed over in silence. Perhaps what is significant is that one is aware that in writing, trying to describe in words the problem of words is a major source of error and sustenance of a degrading image of communication. So often we think to produce something to say, something that is a direction but not an evidence. It is like giving directions without any points of reference. Finally all directions without reference points bring one back to the original spot.

This thought brings to mind the feeling that exists in sixteenth-century English poetry. Here the language was enhanced by the poets' use of the act of writing as a source in the construction of the poem. Many of the words meant things relating to the act of writing as well as to other acts and so the reader became a confidant in the process and thereby consciously participated in the process of reading. How often we are asked to step back and be the receivers of a finished object, although it is an illusion to think this since the words or thoughts must be organized in mind or else not at all. I often think that we ought to call reading translating, and writing also.

The inadvertent is certainly the most profound of the effects of our acts and since it is such, we should take less seriously this endless streaming toward more and more rational formulation of purpose. You mention that art provides a means to unhinge the short arcs of rationality and bring back the respect of the continuous processing of experience. Yet all writing or action is art. Only in the organization of its presentation does it shift. We say "I mean it" when something we have said is considered in another context from the one intended. Identifying art and artists I think makes a subtle sacrifice to the reification we all seem to want relief from. Either we are all artists and we need to perceive ourselves and encourage ourselves as such or else we are none of us artists and the ones that pose as such are simply those who say "I mean it" with a slight grin. What we all love in experiences that are labeled *art* is that whatever we need and want to organize out of them we can, and we can compare this with how the organization came to us (the maker's context). It is this comparison that I think we need to support so that the means of expression and not the thoughts themselves begin to be more interesting all around.

The words are read in order and you read them together and think about how often what is said does not reflect the saying and the dreaming. Perhaps we all need to witness our own organizing patterns in comparison with others. The way to enhance this process is to bring the process more clearly to the surface. Like this, like these black lines on a white surface. Dear Page, what I find most intriguing is what does not reflect, which signals do not return. We have been together these short minutes and the touch of your skin allows for a slow and reassuring sense that organization of signs in space is an important part of your presentation. From now on my respect for you will grow in relation to the absence of any objective posture which you might reveal. Sincerely.

Often I stand in the museums to listen as people look at specific works of art that interest me. In this way my understanding grows. I am always pleased when someone says that they could have made that work. This suggests that the idea of organizing hidden and unconscious variables can be considered. Art that is considered easy to do is only considered so because it has expressed something that brings up a profound unspoken aspect of experience. Technically sophisticated work reveals a distance that can be appreciated but not embraced. Whitehead advocated seeking simplicity and distrusting it. I would advocate seeking the simple access to complexity and attempting to sustain it and reflect upon it. When the words mention you, that is when you cease to exist. Only in processing and thinking out from self is there self. Identified emptiness is all around.

Portraits abound in art not because of the faces but because any organization of experience is a portrait of the person in and of his environment. We describe an animal and then its environment, and what we are portraying is our means to descriptions, our environment in mind.

In our means of communicating we create the models by which we can perceive. When we write and speak we need to be able to involve and interact with metamessages and other means so that the present in the communication is respected. By looking at how we talk or how we read or how we write we do not nullify the importance of the conscious expression but we relegate it to a more appropriate area of description. Without thinking in this way the perpetuation of the problem exists in the communication although derided in the content. This tension seems to aggravate the situation and not help it. It seems so rare that this type of perception finds its way into the words and the way they are presented. We may talk of love forever but by talking of it we fill the time with its absence.

You talk about levels of learning—proto, deutero, and so forth. Since this analysis is retrospective and since a discussion of how one learns requires the acceptance of a learner separated from the observer, I am not sure that there is any edge there. Isn't that just like an ego/superego structuring? If I mention a word like *environment* and then say that describing it is simply a method of observing and has no relationship to the actual, since the division does not exist but is only a means we use to study, then I am working in a progressive and reified structure of communication. The discovery of theories of learning seems to be so alien to the nature of the descriptions and thinking that proceeds in much of your other communications. Perhaps the reification is a reflection of the attempt to correct the program of learning that produces that type of hierarchy and division. To say that I learn something assumes that I know the way I learned it and therefore I have a way to alter not only the learning but the method of learning. By describing it in this way I lose the immediacy of perception. I also would be pushing into the conscious, rational aspects of communication those aspects which seem more related to the whole of my experience—rather than simply just learning. I say I know and that assumes I know I know, which assumes I know that I know I know, and so on. It reminds me of John Donne's "The Triple Fool":

> I am two fooles, I know,
> For loving, and for saying so,
> In whinning poetry:

The reversion to hierarchies of learning structures seems too remote from perception of context and perception of the importance of including the implications of thinking in the process of dynamic interaction. To be able to perceive that there are multiple levels of intention in communication is the evidence not only of sophistication but respect and acceptance of the interactive nature of the environment and therefore of the nature of the self/environment.

To amend an idea is to begin a process that must in some way relate to a double bind. In fact, it occurs that all purposive linguistic statements require a double bind structure. I implore you to understand this also suggests you cannot and you must not question the illusory nature of my request. This is a participatory statement. You can read it and understand it but it requires you to accept something which is not true and to respond to it as if it was. Any situation, in fact, that has a content other than the expression of form in which the content denies the action expressed by the form is what you call a double bind. The interesting aspect is the rational description that engages attention while the bind is in fact working. The subtle level at which it is operating is so devastating that it is completely passed over in most conversations, communications. Last night the president spoke and then the commentators told the public what the president meant. And then the newspaper told the public what the commentators meant. Gregory Bateson wrote a book and if I explored and explained it and what he meant, I would, in fact, be setting up a double bind and one that is so acceptable at most points that it is not even considered. Perhaps the climate of rational discussion is the limiting factor in a withdrawal from this method of control and destruction. It is important to realize the nature of a double bind but perhaps it is more important to act on the structuring of it in one's sensitivity to the communication in which one participates. How can you find an idea if the context in which it is placed is the denial of its actual usefulness as a paradigm of recognition? If the paradigm of double bind worked to release understanding then it would not be couched itself as an example of a double bind.

It is so important to me that the evidence of ideas is in the form in which they are expressed rather than simply in the words of their description. No one has enough energy and consciousness to fight off the inroads made in thinking when the scrutiny of thought made by people who are obviously thinking does not include the means of communication itself. Your eyes are following this argument in series.

There is an essential comment to be made. Every step I make into the rational description and discussion in which I am engaged is a step toward cataloging ideas that can be used as the basis for further discussion but which stop the process at the moment. That is, refining an idea and stating it—writing it down—stops its progress as an expanding, disappearing, reappearing aspect of my processing. What stating an idea does is to leave a remnant at the boundary of your skin which you can or cannot utilize as a stimulus to the continuation of your thinking. However, without remarking that this process, when finished with this process in mind, can enable my processing to continue would be an evidence of my failure to behave according to my own operational principles, which are only clearly felt and become conscious only on application. The poem in mind is the poem on paper.

We walk in the forest of words and see shapes. Later these shapes become letters and their organization words, and their organization becomes sentences and their organization becomes thoughts and so on. The black on the white has not physically changed. The black on the white has physically changed since it only exists as a signaling property in my experience (that *my* now refers to you).

We learn to read and then the single letters and words become habitual to the extent that we see them in their context and not as separate things. When we forget ourselves as a word we exist more fully as our entire context. Negating self does not mean destroying the basis of self, but expanding it to include more than simply the rational and conscious formulation. When someone is accused of negating someone else, that refers to their insistence that the other person's behavior has not succeeded in providing a broad enough base of confidence. Someone who negates others is affirming their conscious and rational aspects and denying to himself access to their varied experiential context. Gregory Bateson does not exist in words nearly as much as I assume he exists outside of them. We must thank Adam and let him go. Chuang Tzu says that he would like to find a man who has forgotten how to use words so that he could have a word with him. I am writing you this letter and feeling the whole time that the words are building in one direction that our experience will only enhance.

How to advocate the absence of reification in a form that reifies. How to advocate the elimination of the division of entities in a format in which this is the basic act performed. The limits of language exist only for the expository type of writing. When the words are arranged to propose a different type of use, then the possibilities expand. Poetry is not simply the singing of a song. It is the realization that we constantly need to reinvent verbal discourse with changed format and changes in content. A poem is a content that seeks to include aspects that are not in the rational or conscious parts of experience. Poetry is in the present. Prose advances the past and tries to control the future. That sentence is certainly an example of what I mean. Embarking on reading we can propose a new stance for the writer only by demonstration not by description. We are working in mind and in body and yet we credit the mind with more consciousness. But your hands are holding the paper, the book, and your eyes are moving over the words and you are sitting most likely and your body needs to dream of running and yet the words flow on. The implication of this is not to stop writing or to condemn rational and verbal discourse to a minor role. The implication is to place this verbal process that has slipped to being a dramatic and important force in our lives without recognition, into a new and more expansive context. Remove the short arc of the rational not only in content but in context. Reread that line and this one. Who is commanding whom? Only you know.

And where is the desire for power gone? How can I control

you and make you understand something? I never could, but could seduce you with words to ignore the context of those words. You have always been in power, if only to the extent of negating yours in favor of someone else's. Following is not passive.

Nothing is passive and is the only aspect that is. When you are encouraged to be active it means that you are encouraged to include your entire contextual development consciously. When you forget something, it is you forgetting, not it. Passive acts are simply a different kind of conscious act—ones with the pronouns diverted. How many times can the *I* be assaulted before assuming invisibility? The importance of dialogue is not in its results but in the nature of its process. I hope you are here.

Systems can operate toward maximization or optimization. Maximization requires competitive analysis and optimization requires complementary analysis. We need to begin to witness the value of the complementary so that we are optimizing all systems and not advocating the maximization of one over another. It is an obvious change in our perception to see the entire context as a complete and dynamic but not progressing system in which we all participate to experience the enhancement of the comprehension of beauty. As in any dynamic and closed system, there are aspects of it that are increasing in scope and activity and aspects of it that are diminishing. This is essential but what is important is to accept these as special cases that are not to be considered the overall motive of activity and planning. The words seek to explain and describe certain ideas that are steps in the overall process but not toward anything except the movement toward a fuller and more acceptable understanding of our self/environment. The words also express the realization of the mind of the reader as the processor of the evidence and not of objective reality. Progress toward a goal is a metastructure that supports the diminution of attention to the moment and allows for thinking to occur that could not be accommodated if the present was considered. These words are being read or not and the continuity of experience exists as I am writing and nowhere else. Reading is again translation.

In an environment, you wrote, for change to occur to one aspect of it without a corresponding change in the overall environment would jeopardize the continuance of the change itself. In any communication network, if one aspect switches the use of words, the others must accommodate if the context of communication is to continue. As in the genotypic change of an organism, the change must allow for the homeostasis to continue or else the change is pathogenic. Any change that does not allow for somatic adaptation denies its effectiveness and the environment's response to it. You suggest another extension into self/environment that is essential. We must see that the environment and the genotypic alteration are all one system and not two aspects, and as we begin to see this, evolution becomes ever more interesting a description. From now on I will use verbs and not nouns. Doing this as a rule without setting up the environment for an adaptation makes communication impossible and so the words pass in order with no possible response. Discourse is at first about the rules of discourse and since this is the case, the rules are expressed in the mode of discourse and cannot be shifted within the frame of the present communication. The only sentence in this paragraph that is not of it is the one about the noun-verb shift. Rules without response and without sensitivity to the entire context stand alone.

A story. Once the environment was considered as everything outside of the body of a human being. The environment was the place where things happened. A stone was pushed off a log and it fell and the falling was a new piece of information that could be compared to what a stone did when it was still. Slowly it became interesting to think of all the other things the stone could do and what this reflected was an awareness of the doing that human beings were capable of. Then the action of the stone and the activity of pushing it became laws and experiments. Later the entire process was made into a small and comprehensible model and all the states of the stone that were possible were considered as either "yes" or "no" states. Then the process of describing created the thing described although the stone and the log were still there. Later the model and the description and the stone and the log and the activity of pushing became part of one entire process and the environment disappeared and the people disappeared and what remained was a dynamic description and series of events without the divisions and nominal relationships.

A poem.

> There were no letters
> there were no numbers
> then there were 26 letters
> and ten numbers. And then
> we wondered where the rest
> of the numbers and letters were
> and the statement of this wonder
> became the evidence of them
> and us.

When we make a story and when we make a poem we have the luxury of a context that exists at multiple levels of aggregation although the crossing from one to the other requires an entirely new set of logics and an entirely new way of observing and expressing. Perhaps beneath all the descriptions you make is the awareness that this is the case and that we have traveled along with our descriptions until this point, where we need to begin to develop new methods of defining, describing, observing, and communicating so that the shift in levels, the shift in awareness of the interaction of the levels, and the interplay but separateness of them, is made useful.

Just as technology is a pathway to differences, our thinking opens new sets of differences from these pathways and we have not as yet determined how to deal with the variations and restrictions that evolve from this perception. Context and self, environment and mind, these are slices of the experience of living that transpose easily but also confuse with seeming preciseness. The ecology is an ecology of mind, and to express the need to describe it this way suggests that the attention is not with the process but with the now-identified things as they are. We make changes that cannot threaten our continuity and so point to where we want to go although we are not there yet. The thinking that you have described sits at an edge of an experience that does not have any mapping techniques yet and so our desire is not matched by our skills. Yet in being aware of the problem we begin to stretch and reorder how and why we think and act as we do. The stimulus of thinking in this way is similar to the way you describe carbon dioxide's function in the context of breathing. It is a sign that the homeostasis is threatened but it does not threaten the entire being. We ask to develop a sense of the interactive relation between self and environment knowing that those two parts are only one and that we have divided them up only to be able to join them into one dynamic understanding. We write in series and inevitably build up expectations toward a progression so that at the end the whole is revealed even though we know the need to have complementary systems and nonprogressive methods of action. We look at the effects that human beings have had on the environment only when we consider ourselves not part of it and them. Then we realize that it is exactly because we do not think of ourselves as part of it and them that we can behave and think as we do. The major mysteries are those that we continue to pursue and the methods of pursuing them depict the possibility of arriving at a new place only to discover that it is the same place seen from a different perspective. That we understand the process of living at all makes us hold to it and seek to continue it and thereby live not in the present but in the preparation for the future and in reworking the past. At the moment when we can step into the present completely, the need for these ruminations about how and why will become a sign on a journey we no longer are taking.

Sincerely,
Edwin Schlossberg
Chester, Massachusetts
July 1975

End Linkage: A Tool for Cross-Cultural Analysis

❂ ❂

MARGARET MEAD

Margaret Mead, anthropologist and psychologist, is the author of numerous books dealing with change in our time. Among her recent works are *World Enough: Rethinking the Future* (with Ken Heyman) and her autobiography, *Blackberry Winter: My Earlier Years.* Dr. Mead is curator emeritus of anthropology at the American Museum of Natural History. She lives in New York City.

The particular quality of Gregory Bateson's mind and the way in which he distills ideas from interaction with other people, which they in turn can distill again, is hard to describe. It is closely related to the ideas themselves, for his most exciting ideas, schismogenesis (Bateson, G., 1936a), the double bind (Bateson, G., 1972a), and the relationship of purposeful human behavior to linear systems (Bateson, M. C., 1972) have all been about relationships between individuals or groups of individuals, elaborated and stylized by experience or culture. He has always emphasized that thinking grows from thinking, and that "some data going through the system" is necessary but that nevertheless it is not the nature of the data itself, but the process of mulling it over, sometimes very loosely, sometimes with extraordinary detail and precision, that provides the next step. And he has also recognized that there is little chance of predicting where the next idea might come from: It might be from a request to give a paper on a subject about which he previously thought very little, or from watching the behavior of his own child, from some detail of a ceremony, or—later—from the responses of the schizophrenic patients with whom he and his associates were working (Bateson, G., et al., 1956). The only constant in the process was his own continuing curiosity about a series of themes—meta-themes—which have preoccupied him from his earliest work to his latest. Meanwhile, those of us who worked with him have participated in the process of developing a particular idea and taken it to use further in our own work. These by-products of the process of interactive thought have only a limited interest for Bateson himself; they cast light on the fertile fields of his associates' inquiring minds to grow or wither as they may, or to lie dormant for decades until some event brings them to life, as forest fires do for seeds that are encapsulated and unresponsive to rainfall unless first seared by flame.

In this brief article, I propose to trace one of these ideas, which was rather infelicitously labeled "end linkage," and which I have found to be continuingly useful over the thirty-five years since it was first developed. The central idea is closely related to schismogenesis, and consists of constructing a paradigm in which some universal symmetrical or complimentary biological relationship, such as that between parents and children, is shown to be linked in different cultures to different kinds of behavior, which may itself become culturally modified. Thus the biological given that all children are succored by parents is made primary and the accompanying behaviors, such as dominance, submission, exhibitionism, and spectatorship, can be shown to differ in different cultures or in different classes within a culture. The primary paradigm is thus:

> A given relationship, either biological or situational, a series of behaviors that are contrastingly linked to one or the other side of the relationship, so:

English (*middle and upper class*)

PARENTS	CHILDREN
succoring	dependence
dominance	submission
exhibitionism	spectatorship
end linkage	

American (middle class)

PARENTS	CHILDREN
succoring	dependence
dominance (slight)	submission (slight)
spectatorship	exhibitionism

By delineating the way in which types of parental behavior and expected types of filial behavior are stylized in different cultures, it is possible to identify differences between cultures and especially differences that are important in cross-cultural relationships. For example, if the parent role is an exhibitionistic one, as is true in England, the children become the audience for the time being. In the United States, on the other hand, where the child is the exhibitionist and the parent the spectator, the speaker behaves like an American child, shouting and boasting with all the rights of the small over and against the larger and stronger. English speakers, using a calm, parental tone, seem arrogant to American audiences and American speakers seem boastful or obstreperous to the English. The English speaker makes his points by understatement, being self-deprecatory in the major clause, and reserving the punch line, which asserts his superiority, for the subordinate clause. The American speaker, like his child prototype, overstates in order to get the attention of an audience assumed to be as unwilling to listen as his parents once were when he was asserting his childish achievements.

Such relationships, linked by cultural expectation, may be followed from society to society, outlining both expectations and sources of cross-national misunderstandings.

1933

This specific formulation grew out of observations of our two-year-old daughter, the behavior of her English nurse, parallel observations of two English children who came to live with us during the war, and discussions between Gregory

Bateson, Geoffrey Gorer, and myself in the winter of 1941–42 about Anglo-American differences. The first complete discussion, published as "Morale and National Character," Chapter Five of the 1942 Yearbook of the Society for the Psychological Study of Social Issues (Bateson, G., 1942), was primarily thought of as a tool for dealing with problems faced by the United States in its relations with other countries—allies and enemies—at the beginning of World War II. However, before going into more detail on how these ideas were used in broadcasts, public speaking, and conferences, I wish to go back to the earlier roots of the idea—the standardization of contrast in sex roles as it occurred on the Sepik River, where the interrelationship between cultural data and theoretical ideas is particularly clear.

During Christmas of 1932, Gregory Bateson was in the middle of his third trip to the Iatmul people of the Middle Sepik River in New Guinea, and Reo Fortune and I had just left the Mundugumor of the Yuat River, after completing a study of the Arapesh (Mead, 1935). On previous trips, Bateson had been concerned with analogies between homologous and homonymous functions among the Iatmul, seeking relationships between his biological understandings and his cultural data (Bateson, G., 1932). He came to a kind of temporary dead end, and was going through a period of dutifully adding to his supply of material but with no conviction as to where it would lead.

I had taken as my principal field problem the cultural standardization of male and female roles, as I believed that we could not begin to discuss what types of behavior were innate, linked to the biologically given rather than to the socially or situationally given, until we had explored the extent to which cultural expectations stylized behavior. Were women innately more submissive, less initiating, less creative, and so forth than men, or were such differences due to the conditions and biology of maternity, or to roles that had been historically assigned? Did men have more drive than women, and if so was this a function of their physique and their endocrine system, their need to compensate for a lesser role in parenthood, or was it merely a matter of cultural assignment of roles?

By Christmas of 1932 we had studied two groups, in which the assignment of personality style had been very little differentiated by sex: Among the Arapesh both men and women were expected to be lightly sexed, parental, cherishing, uninterested in warfare, preoccupied with the values of feeding and growth—behavior which in some societies is attributed to women. Among the Mundugumor, both men and women were highly sexed, actively preoccupied with aggressive activities, uninterested in parenthood values—behavior which in some societies had been attributed to men. It was clear that the historical assignment of personality type could be enormously influenced by culture, but I felt that in a sense all my research to that point had been unilluminating. We already had ample documentation of the enormous differences in behavior that existed between different cultures, and within the same culture at different periods of history. What I was looking for were links between the biologically given and the culturally variable—ways of building a science that took the psychic unity of mankind into account but also allowed for the systematic inclusion of innate differences among individuals and between the sexes.

Ruth Benedict had already developed her basic configurative approach to cultures, which she described as "personality writ large," each culture selectively emphasizing some particular human potentialities that were not, however, related to one another in any systematic way (Mead, 1974a). She had distinguished a polarization between Apollonian and Dionysian cultures, illustrated by Pueblo and Plains Indians, and then placed another emphasis upon paranoid types of thinking, as illustrated by the Dobuans, studied by Reo Fortune (Fortune, 1932) and the Kwakiutl Indians, studied by Franz Boas. The manuscript of her forthcoming book, *Patterns of Culture* (Benedict, 1934), had been sent to Reo Fortune and myself in the autumn of 1932, so that her ideas were available to us when we met with Gregory Bateson. I had already written a section on the personality of the Samoans in *The Social Organization of Manu'a* (Mead, 1930), based on my discussions with Ruth Benedict while she was developing her theoretical position. This was essentially a description of what Bateson came to call "ethos"—the stylization of affective behavior—as he formulated it in *Naven.* But at that point it was not clear what Ruth Benedict meant, or what I was searching for, in looking for the way in which the biological origins of something vaguely called "personality" was only modified by culture. When Ruth Benedict asked the question, "Would I have been happy in another culture—Egypt perhaps?" she was making an assumption about a part of herself that was innate and significant (Mead, 1959). When I puzzled over contrasts between myself and most of the highly motivated career women I knew, I was trying to identify ways in which sex was not a sufficient explanation even for attitudes toward childbearing. Meanwhile, in his earlier work on dreams Reo Fortune had been searching for psychological regularities that could be treated as systematic, universal functions of the human psyche.

During the first months of 1933, Reo Fortune and I worked among the Tchambuli of Chambri Lake, while Gregory Bateson continued his research among the Iatmul. Bateson was struck by the Iatmuls' theatrical emphasis upon women as submissive—dramatized by Naven ceremonies during which the mother's brother assumes widows' dirty weeds—on one hand, and the contrasting ceremonial emphasis, where the father's sister plays the conspicuous role of a magnificent, strutting, malelike figure on the other. Meanwhile I was finding among the Tchambuli just the cultural contrast that I needed, for while the women dressed up the men and children, they themselves were unadorned, brisk, businesslike, and the men devoted their time to aesthetic pursuits, self-ornamentation, and displaying the personality type that our own culture would have characterized as feminine.

In discussing the contrasts and likenesses between the Tchambuli and the Iatmul—who were culturally closely related—and the extent to which various culturally determined sex-typed behaviors appeared to the three of us who were actively observing them, we began to work out a set of formulations about sex and temperament. We developed the hypothesis that there was a similar range of temperaments, with male and female versions, in every culture, and that any one culture might stylize both males and females as belonging to the same temperament, as the Arapesh and Mundugumor had done, or assign one of the recurrently available temperaments to males and another to females. In the first case, the difference in the culturally stylized behavior of men and women would be small and limited to the exercise of primary sex functions and to the most basic division of labor based on assumed differences between men and women in strength, mobility, and suitability for combat. In the second case, illustrated by both the Iatmul and Tchambuli, the contrasts expected between the sexes would be accentuated by an expected difference in temperament: Among the Iatmul the women were regarded as submissive and realistic; men were expected to be theatrical, harsh and exhibitionistic. The Tchambuli, by demonstrating the reverse of Euro-American cultural expectations, emphasized our developing hypotheses even more. Going further, and using cultures and individuals we had known, we developed a preliminary statement of the relationship between culture and personality as we saw how different cultures selected among different temperaments the stylizations for the behavior of the sexes of different classes or castes (Mead, 1972).

When we left the Sepik River in May 1933, I went home to the United States to write *Sex and Temperament,* and Gregory Bateson began the work that was to become *Naven.* In his initial presentation of the Naven theme, at the International Congress of Anthropological and Ethnological Sciences in the summer of 1934 (Bateson, G., 1934), he examined the stylization of sex-attributed personality traits by discussing ritual transvestism in unorthodox situations, such as times of mourning. We both also investigated the existing studies of constitutional types, Kretschmer's particularly (Kretschmer, 1925), but this investigation stands in *Naven* rather like a plum in a pudding, because Bateson had already turned away from his interest in temperament to questions of the theoretical implications of interaction styles. *Naven* then appeared as a book about thinking and about social processes, not a book about the relationships between innate temperament and culture or contrastive sex roles, although these were, of course, the subject matter of the Naven ceremony. We worked on the relationship between temperament and culture in the earlier phases of *Naven,* but these were no longer at the center of Bateson's interest, although they remained available for later thought.

The selection of Bali for further fieldwork after our marriage in 1936 had been based upon the expectation that Bali presented a culture that would help to enlarge our hypotheses about universally prevalent temperaments. Although Bali proved useful, our interests were highly theoretical; Bateson's were expressed later in "Bali, the Value System of a Steady State" (Bateson, G., 1949), and mine were concentrated on the intensive study of the processes by which a particular cultural character—compound of temperament, cultural child rearing practices and idiosyncratic ingredients—was developed (Bateson, G., and Mead, 1942).

1940–1943

It was not until we addressed ourselves to the wartime problems of cross-cultural understanding and morale building, that we again used the earlier style of thinking that had originated in culturally elaborated contrasts between the sexes, with sex as a biological given and cultures as the variable. I was asked to take part in a half-hour radio broadcast to demonstrate that race did not matter and culture did. In preparing for this broadcast, Bateson began elaborating on his observations of the difference between British and American linkage of exhibitionism with the parental and child roles respectively. We found a gifted script writer, a young Englishman who subsequently went to Harvard, and who with very little instruction developed five scripts: an American breakfast table, an English breakfast table, a German breakfast table (where the child was required to exhibit submission as opposed to exhibiting independence as in the American scene), and two breakfast tables that demonstrated how children of Chinese descent could be Americanized. The thinking that went into the development of the end linkage paradigm was spelled out in the chapter for the *Yearbook on Civilian Morale* (Bateson, G., 1942). I took the substance and the theoretical formulation of the broadcast with me when I went to England as a wartime lecturer, and the formulation proved so accurate that I could select illustrations from the behavior of chairmen, speakers, and audiences wherever I went (Mead, 1944).

Although the emphasis in the initial formulation was upon symmetrical or complementary relationships between two groups, parents and children, Bateson had already included the possibility of ternary relationships, such as child-mother-nurse in England; younger pupil, the scholarly head boy, and the athlete who enforces the rules in school; and the private, the officer, and the sergeant in the army. These refinements proved useful in exploring the difficulties the British had in forming a female army corps until the appropriate type of sergeant to fill the third position in the officer-private relationship was found.

While Bateson did no more with this theme, another possible product of the end linkage formulation appeared when Geoffrey Gorer and I substituted a common situation for a given biological relationship in analyzing the contrast in British and American ideas of partnership (Mead, 1947, 1948). Both peoples used the simile that we were partners in the great war against Nazism, but different formulations of partnership led to endless confusion. The British used a tennis game as their model: The partners were assumed to be equal for the duration of the game and it was their duty to boast and grieve for one another—"Hard luck, partner!" "Well shot, partner!" For the Americans, the model was a business partnership between unequals: typically one provided the capital, the other the brains. Partnerships were not for a stated duration and could only be dissolved with discomfort; partners did not boast for each other, but each explained privately that the other would have been helpless without him. When Churchill said to his partner the American: "Give us the tools and we'll finish the job," his assumption of equal status was misread by Americans as an expression of the superiority of the British. And when the British boasted of their American partners, and congratulated the Americans on the antiaircraft guns that had saved Britain, they were affronted to find that instead of replying with some courteous "Well shot, partner!" and praise for the Normandy landing platforms, the Americans simply blazoned the British praise of our antiaircraft guns throughout the American press. This use of a recurrent situation, like partnership, was to come in again later, in other applications of the original end linkage idea. I used it in formulating the role of the mother in American culture in *And Keep Your Powder Dry* (Mead, 1942). The small boy must always show that combat was initiated by another for the benefit of the mother who gives him conflicting directions: "I didn't think my little boy would hit another little boy," and "Well, why did you let him take it away from you? You're as big as he is. Go and get it back!" The development of the American's insistence that he never initiates hostilities, only puts a chip on his shoulder for someone else to knock off, can be related to the fact that the mother has to develop behavior in her son that she does not herself exemplify.

1945–1950

The themes in *And Keep Your Powder Dry* were worked out in discussions with Gregory Bateson and Geoffrey Gorer. Some possibilities for this type of analysis were elaborated by Geoffrey Gorer in his discussion of the female conscience and the role of the female schoolteacher in *The American People*

(Gorer, 1948), and in his subsequent illuminating study of the changes brought about in British attitudes toward law and order by the invention of the English police (Gorer, 1955), modeled upon the paternal and protective role of the English county magistrate. All of the first policemen chosen by Sir Robert Peel were big, patient men who could be trusted not to retaliate and to preserve order unarmed.

When the study of Japanese national character was begun, one interesting example of the miscarriage of communication occurred. In a memorandum to the United States Department of State in early 1942, written by Gorer and presented in the name of the Committee for National Morale, it was recommended that the United States refrain from attacking the Japanese emperor as he would be needed at the end of the war—a prophetic recommendation which events proved correct—and there was also a propagandistic recommendation suggesting that "The United States should adopt a firm fatherly tone toward the Japanese" (Gorer, 1942). This was misinterpreted by the Office of the Coordinator of Information in a broadcast to Japan stating that "The United States is your father." After an initial sense of despair over ever being able to communicate in a useful way, we realized that the error was ours. There is no "firm fatherly tone" in the United States such as Geoffrey Gorer, as an Englishman, had wished to evoke. The best we could have done to carry out Gorer's intent would have been to say, "Talk to the Japanese as if they are fourth graders and you are fifth."

In the original discussions that led to the formulation of symmetrical and complementary schismogenesis, and later to end linkages, there was some thought to the way in which such analyses illuminated relationships among different social classes, how aristocracy and peasantry might be united in the support of the same ethos, both alienated from the middle class, and how the lower middle class occupied a special position as the class which had to react to the contradictory attitudes of those below them, who aspired to reach their status, and those above them, who viewed the possibility of falling to their status as totally abhorrent. Here, as in the discussion of the American mother who gives her son contradictory messages, there are glimpses of Bateson's later formulation of the double bind (Bateson, G., 1972b).

As we continued to use these insights in subsequent discussions of relationships between nations and nationals of different countries, the emphasis shifted somewhat to the parent-child model as being one of strength and weakness. In Britain strength is openly acknowledged and is the basis for action, so that the British version of compromise is of the strong graciously acceding to the weak; whereas Americans, always seeing themselves as weaker, feel they have lost even if they gain 90 percent of their points. This difference in the attribution of initiative to either the parent or child position shows up sharply in attitudes toward bullying: Both British and Americans repudiate bullying, but where the older boy in Britain sees himself as the surrogate of the strong father, the older boy in the United States sees his autonomy threatened by the weaker younger brother, who is protected by the mother. This accounts for the extraordinary distortions in reality that made it possible in the spring of 1975 for American manhood to be restored by the pitiful Mayaguez incident, during which we confronted the insult offered to us by a tiny, destroyed Cambodia.

The next systematic use of the formulation of end linkage was Natalie Joffe's study, "Non-Reciprocity Among East European Jews" (1949, 1953).

❁ ❁

NON-RECIPROCITY AMONG EAST EUROPEAN JEWS

All of the following remarks apply only to in-group behavior. The obligations enjoined on a Jew not to take interest on a loan, to keep an open house, and to support the various community enterprises do not necessarily function in his relationship to the Gentile world. It would be hard to envisage this society without its operating in a Gentile milieu—it is indeed almost impossible to conceive of its existence without a strong out-group, because its economic base lies in distribution of, and more recently manufacture of, commodities rather than in agriculture.

For a society within the framework of the Western cultural tradition, East European Jewish culture exhibits a minimum of reciprocal behavior. Wealth, learning, and other tangible and intangible possessions are fluid and are channeled so that in the main they flow from the "strong," or "rich," or "learned," or "older," to those who are "weaker," "poorer," "ignorant," or "younger." Therefore all *giving* is downward. This mechanism is conceived of as a way to perpetuate the community and to maintain the status quo, the society never being thrown out of balance through internal crises. All higher status, with the exception of sex, is achieved and achievable, and even sex-typed status (that of husband-father and wife-mother) are achieved categories additional to the ascribed one of sex.

The good things of the world are infinite and acquirable. They are those things which confer higher status and are acquired not for themselves alone but for transmission, and the flow is always from the strong to the weaker—a process that might best be compared to the second law of thermodynamics.

Since Jews do not constitute a land-identified community,* and there is no concept of "retirement" (absolute age always is deferred to), little emphasis is placed upon the common virtue of building up a patrimony or a landed estate to be passed on to one's heirs for the establishment of a dynasty; it is also possible that this position is reinforced by the fact that the vast majority of Jews living under *shtetl* conditions were extremely poor and there was a very slim margin between adequate

* "Jews constitute a 'people-identified' community. The community consists of any ten adult men. It is of interest to note that stars play little part in the orientation and spatial concepts of the Jews." (Comment by Dr. A. I. Hallowell, at a meeting of the American Ethnological Society on "Spatial Recognition in the Psycho-dynamics of a Culture," January 13, 1948.)

support for a family and near-starvation, which allowed practically no latitude for savings; instead, money is more apt to be given to the young people at the time of marriage for the foundation of a new family unit. What remains to be passed on at the time of death is usually minimal—the seat in the synagogue, a pair of candlesticks, some books or jewelry.

To the Jews, even the most orthodox, death is an occasion of unmitigated grief, and all of the reminders of the bereavement are disposed of as soon as possible. (In New York, for example, it is usual for the family of the deceased to move as soon as possible from the apartment where the death occurred.) The clothing of the dead person is *given* away, not thrown away or sold. There seems to be some idea that cloth, being soft and permeable, has some of the personality of the dead person, and it is disrespectful for the members of the immediate family to think that they can fill it. Metal, being hard, is less liable to be imbued with this aura, so jewelry is saved and worn, as are household effects. Heirlooms like a samovar or candlesticks are valued, for they show that the family in the past was rich enough to have them; but there are few of them.

It is mandatory for the good things of life to be shared or to be passed downward during one's lifetime, so the miser is never respected; instead he is openly criticized, and his behavior is deplored and condemned. It is one of the greatest blessings in the world to put what you have at the service of others, be it wealth, learning, or children. Indeed, the concept of the good deed, the *Mitzvah,* is not voluntary—it has been enjoined upon every Jew by God. It is only through these acts that you are assured of entrance into Paradise. These duties are not construed as a burden, but rather as a source of joy. The *Mitzvah* has been so worked into the structure of the society that it serves as a channel through which property, learning, and the like are diffused downward. For example, it is a *Mitzvah* for a wealthy man to marry off an orphan girl, so he furnishes her with a dowry, negotiates for the marriage and supplies the wedding feast. Or fostering of learning is a *Mitz-*

vah, therefore if you are learned, you expound the Torah to others, or, failing that, support the seminary. To take money for such acts has a low prestige affect, which may explain why the *Malamed* (teacher) is despised.

It is shameful, however, to receive succor of any sort from those who are inferior to you in any status. To receive any of the aforementioned implies that you are in a position to be controlled, for the reciprocal of the downward-giving is deference. Children must defer to adults, the young to the old, the ignorant to the learned, women to men. To accept things means that you are inferior to the donor, which may in part explain the contempt the Jews have for those who take bribes, because, by acceptance, they become "subadult." It is not shameful to accept from your *equals*—it is preferred. This may cast light on the fact that the old prefer to live in squalor, where they can be "their own bosses," rather than with children who can supply creature comforts, or favor living in a home for the aged rather than to be beholden to an individual.

The following lists illustrate (1) some points of transmission from those of higher status (donors) to those of lower status (recipients) and some forms of deferent behavior expected of the latter; and (2) some points of symmetical behavior, give and take between equals. Types of donor-recipient relationships are summarized in Chart A.

1. Points of Transmission; Donors and Recipients

MITZVAH (good deeds)	DEFERENCE
I. Adult to child, older to younger	I. Child to adult
a. Support	a. Deference
b. *Hanukah-Gelt*	b. To marry and have children (parental)
c. New holiday clothing	c. To say *Kaddish* (prayers for the dead, primarily for parents)
d. Education and learning	
e. Dowry and marriage	
f. Care for orphans	
g. Mediate ethical standards	

II. Learned to ignorant
   a. Transmission of learning
   b. Accessibility to those who seek to learn
   c. Support of institutions of learning
   d. Settlement of points of law
   e. Mediation between Jews and Gentiles

II. Ignorant to learned
   a. Deference and docility

III. Rich to poor
   a. Support
   b. Free matzoths
   c. Free meals, *kest*
   d. Linens for the newborn
   e. Arrangement of marriage for an orphan
   f. Care of the sick
   g. Burial and care of cemetery
   h. Talmud, Torah, Yeshiva, etc.

III. Poor to rich
   a. Deference

IV. Husband to wife
   a. Support
   b. Assurance that wife will get into Heaven

IV. Wife to husband
   a. Deference
   b. Feeding and caring for husband and children
   c. Working so husband can study
   d. Mediation with mundane world
   e. Supplying husband with *Mitzvahs*

V. Dead to living
  a. Advice in times of crisis
  b. Mediation in the afterworld

V. Living to dead
  a. Burial of the dead
  b. Maintenance of the cemetery
  c. Prayers for the dead (*Kaddish*)

VI. Host to guest
  a. To keep an open house
  b. To feed and care for guests (especially on Sabbath and holidays)

VI. Guest to host

VII. Well to sick
  a. To care for the sick
  b. To offer them things

VII. Sick to well

2. Symmetrical Behavior: Give and Take between Equals

I. WOMAN-WOMAN

a. Exchange of *Schalochmones* (sweetmeats) at Purim; the exchange is calculated not in terms of identity but of unlikes so grouped as to be equated.
b. Mothers-in-law dance together at weddings; mothers-in-law brag to each other.

II. MAN-MAN

a. Care during illness (a temporary condition)
b. Support of the aged
c. The *Minyan*, etc.
d. Burial

CHART A

Points of Transmission: Donors and Recipients

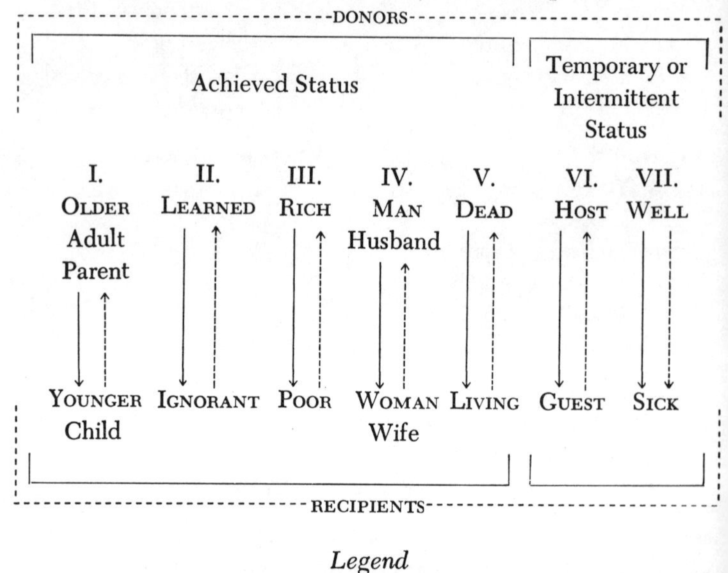

Legend

MITZVAH (GOOD DEEDS) ———

DEFERENCE — —

(Joffe 1949, 1953)

This analysis, in which Natalie Joffe used parent-child, man-wife and situational analyses, proved valuable as background for Mark Zborowski's subsequent study, *People in Pain* (Zborowski, 1969). Many years later I realized the full implication, namely that when Jews who had done large favors for Gentiles asked for small symbolic favors in return, it was their way of avoiding an asymmetrical relationship between parent and child, donor and recipient, and restoring the recipient to equal status.

In the French section of Columbia University Researches in Contemporary Cultures, Rhoda Métraux developed the statement of *Themes in French Culture* (Métraux and Mead, 1954) and incorporated some of Geoffrey Gorer's original statements about dyadic relationships within the foyer. In *The*

Study of Culture at a Distance she expanded the discussion of spectatorship and exhibitionism.

A NOTE ON THE SPECTATOR IN FRENCH CULTURE

Spectatorship and the position of the spectator are highly stylized in French culture. Whereas *looking* is regarded by the Chinese, for example, as an active occupation and by Americans as a passive one, it seems to have the double possibility for the French. Spectatorship in French culture may be active, as in the case of the critic who passes judgment on what he sees; or it may be passive, as in the case on the one hand of the apprentice who learns by watching the performance of a master, or on the other hand of the person who is involuntarily prevented from participating in what he sees.

Involuntary non-participation in what is seen provides a dramatic theme in which the problem may be resolved in opposite ways: (1) the passive spectator (e.g., an unattractive or helpless older man watches a younger man with a woman to whom he himself is attracted; a young man watches an experienced older man with a woman to whom he himself is attracted; a woman watches her husband with a younger daughter-like girl; a girl watches a sister with a man to whom she herself is attached, etc.) may enter into hopeless, destructive, or self-destructive rivalry with the person whose place he (or she) would like to take;* or (2) the spectator may, on the

* Among recent French films in which this theme has been explored, cf. *Les Enfants du Paradis, Le Silence Est d'Or, Le Corbeau, Panique, Marie du Port,* etc. The theme of the spectator in French films has been treated extensively by Martha Wolfenstein and Nathan Leites in "Plot and Character in Selected French Films: An Analysis of Fantasy" (Métraux and Mead, 1954).

contrary, be stimulated to re-enact what has been seen—or the suggested possibilities—with another, more available person.*

Both of these situations, it would seem, derive from the spectatorship characteristic of the learner; in both, the spectator—like the apprentice—is in a subordinate position to those who are seen. When this brings about a reversal of expected roles—i.e., an individual who is normally in a superordinate position is made to be a passive spectator—this may be an essential tragic (or sometimes comic) element in the situation.

The active spectator, in contrast, is regularly in a superordinate position; that he does not necessarily act out his role is then a matter of his own choice. So, for instance, as an active spectator, the critic compares what he sees—the novel, the painting, the actor, etc.—with standard or model productions, acting in this respect as the mentor of the artist who may be an innovator; at the same time he instructs the passive audience—the general public—in how to see the work of art or the actor's style, and so on, and how to place it in its context of other work.†

There is also a third possible position for the spectator in French culture: that of the onlooker who voluntarily abstains from participation in that he withholds the expression of judgment and affect—the laissez-faire position of the mature individual who observes *la vie humaine* without commitment or comment. The problems of this position, in terms of intellec-

* This possibility is used repeatedly with comic effect in French films. So, for instance, a young man may be shown watching an attractive woman singing on a stage; he then turns to kiss his sweetheart. It is also used in French advertisements, where looking may be combined (e.g., in advertisements for perfumes and foods) with another kind of sensory experience.

† See, for example, the discussion of the function of criticism by the French critic Henri Peyre (1944). The artist himself may, however, reverse the position of the critic, as when an informant, a French-trained artist, comments that "critics were always hanging around the artists' cafés, trying to find out what it was all about, so they would know what to write." (Unpublished document RCC-F 210.)

tual and affective commitment, have been explored by various writers (Sartre, de Beauvoir, Camus, etc.) in recent years.* As a possible position for the mature individual, voluntary non-participating spectatorship must be paired with one position of exhibitionism—that of the superordinate individual who is looked at, but who does not, ideally, take part in action (e.g., the President of the French Republic).†

The two types of active and passive spectatorship first described suggest that there are in French culture two forms of actor-spectator relationship, and that these involve a reversal of superordination and subordination and a different definition of "spectatorship" and "exhibitionism" for each type. The third type (with its non-participating exhibitionist opposite) suggests the importance in French culture of situations in which non-participation (in the sense of overt expression of feeling, etc.) is a form of regularly expected behavior.

With this in mind, we may now turn to the *foyer* and to the relationship between parent and child in the home to look for models of the actor-audience bipolarity. French relationships tend to be of an exclusive dyadic nature; tend, that is, to be relationships between pairs of individuals. Geoffrey Gorer has described the *foyer* as follows:**

> A married couple, together with their children, constitute a *foyer*, a *foyer* consists of a nexus of dyadic relationships—relationships between pairs of individuals—each of which by its existence gives strength, richness, and significance to the others. All relationships tend to be of an exclusive dyadic nature; valued emotional complexity develops in those situa-

* Nathan Leites (1947) has discussed a special aspect of the problem in connection with his analysis of Camus's *L'Etranger*. (Leites, in Mead and Métraux, 1953, Part V.)

† An understanding of both aspects of this position is essential to any discussion of contemporary French neutralism in international politics.

** Unpublished document RCC-F 123. For a detailed description of expected French family relationships, cf. Métraux and Mead (1953).

tions where the whole group are interconnected through mutual relations over a long stretch of time.

Thus in discussing relationships in the *foyer,* one must consider not only the pair who make up any one dyad, but also the expected relationship of the third person to a dyad, and vice versa (i.e., on the one hand, the pairs of husband-wife, mother-son, father-son, etc.; on the other hand, the relationship of son to mother-father, of mother to father-son, etc.).

In the earliest relations of parent and child in the family, the father's role is almost entirely one of distant spectatorship, with the major interaction that of mother and child.* It is the mother who "teaches" the child to learn (to be receptive and responsive) and who, when the child is still too young to talk, may respond in its stead so that it is provided not only with models of initiative (the adult position) but also of response (the child's position). As the child gains in autonomy, it learns better to respond—rather than (as is expected of the American child, for instance) to experiment and explore on its own behalf. Therefore it learns also to expect that initiation and response are paired. Learning is acquired by repeatedly following the correct models provided by elders who have the skills, and understanding is expected to follow upon, rather than to be a necessary condition to, learning. This especially emphasizes the passive position of the learner, the apprentice. Later, when the child no longer requires nursery care, a special relationship may develop between father and son† and, still later, if the daughter is "*chic et caline,*" between father and daughter, to both of which the mother is a spectator.

But, most important, the child is expected to be a quiet spectator of the interaction between father and mother.

* This is, of course, not peculiar to the French family.

† French male informants seldom speak of having had an intimate relationship to their father, but such an early relationship may prefigure the later one between teacher and student, etc. In French autobiographies (Gide, Loti, etc.), it is the breaking-off of such an early affectionate relationship, viewed retrospectively after the death of the father, that is sometimes regarded as particularly significant.

("Father" and "mother" are used here advisedly, as the child is excluded from various aspects of the marital relationship. So, for instance, both the parents' sexual relationship and their discussions of financial problems and plans are kept from children. As one woman informant said: "When you speak of the *family*, you say 'father' and mother'" [not 'husband' and 'wife'].) At table, when the child eats with its parents, it is told: "*Mange et tais-toi*"—"Eat and be quiet"—while the parents converse and, through their conversation, provide the child with a model for the enjoyment of food.

Later, the school child may be called upon by the parents to perform for them (especially for the father), or it may be included to a certain extent in conversation, where, again, it exhibits what it has learned. In such situations the parents (especially the father, with the mother providing a link between the two—both supporting the father and protecting the child) become the spectators of the child's activity. But unlike the child who is learning and who is expected to be a noncritical spectator, the parents as spectators judge the child's performance—comparing the child not to other actual children but to what the child should be becoming.*

Thus, briefly, the two positions of spectatorship are built up in the family, one based on the child learning by watching its parents (and by responding to them), the other based on the parents' (especially the father's) watching the learned behavior of the child and responding to its exhibition with praise or criticism.

Returning now to the position of the uninvolved spectator, we may also consider the "outsider" to any of the dyads. In fact, the dyadic relationships of the *foyer* are such that the "outsider" himself is involved in an exclusive relationship with each of the members of any dyad and he is an "outsider" only

* French informants regularly emphasize that each child in the family is (or should be) treated differently from the others—one being given adult books to read, the other not, at the same age, etc. —in terms of personality differences. (Such statements must be regarded as retrospective comments on what the child desired as well as on what may have happened.) —(Métraux, 1953)

to the extent that each dyad has its area of privacy, of interests and information, of feeling and comment, not shared with others. And the security of everyone depends upon the area of privacy being maintained by all. Thus each individual is at some time a spectator who is expected not to intrude upon, not to comment upon, the activities of another pair of individuals. The assumption is not that he will not have his private views and feelings, but rather that he will not air them in such a way that the relationship between another pair is threatened or disturbed. For, as visualized by the French, the danger of intrusion comes not from within but from outside the closed circle of the family. (But the pathology of looking is undoubtedly based upon such unauthorized looking and being looked at.)

Thus the patterned relationships in the *foyer* and, among these, the relationship of parent and child, provide us with one set of models for the several positions of the spectator in French culture. Further elaboration would require examination of other linked relationships systematically related to these family models.

We continued to elaborate on these ideas in the post–World War II years. In 1963 I developed the strong and weak and the situational theme further in a manual prepared for the World Federation for Mental Health, "The Selection of Personnel for International Service."

LATER APPLICATIONS TO INTERNATIONAL RELATIONS

The factor of culture has to be taken into account at every stage in the selection and training of personnel for cross-cultural work. The culture in which a candidate has been reared, the culture in which he will work, the cultures from which other members of the team are drawn, and the culture within which the particular bureaucratic procedure or ethic of international work originated or by which it was principally shaped, must all be considered.

Ideally it should be possible to establish a series of indicators that vary from culture to culture and are of different degrees of relevance and particularity that would make it possible to compute by machine the probability of success or failure of any group of individuals whose cultural backgrounds are known. Any such set of indicators would apply only to the cultural factor and would have to be combined with other factors, chiefly the situational-historical factors such as history of past contacts of the same sort; extent of carryover from a past contact situation of antagonisms or sympathies (e.g., from previous colonialism); presence of a racial factor; extent of stereotyping (of all Caucasians, or Protestants, or Northern Europeans, or Latin Americans) by the host population or particular bureaucracy.

These two factors, the cultural and the situational-historical, will sometimes overlap. If there has been a long history of political or commercial contact between two national groups, the stereotypes may be quite close to the cultural facts. Examples are Indian experience of British ethics of fairness to the underdog; British experience of the Burmese ability to play the different contenders for monopoly position off against each other; Netherlands experience with the status-bound conservatism of Eurasian civil servants which developed during Netherlands rule in the East Indies.

At the other extreme, in some small bureaucratic units of a large organization in which many nationalities are represented, a fortunate or unfortunate experience with a single individual —a lone Hungarian or Egyptian or Venezuelan—may color the response of the other members of the team to all others of the same national group in ways that are slightly or perhaps not at all related to the culture involved. A full knowledge of any international working situation would include such historical features, especially those which are based on a long period of contact and are thus regularized and predictable.

Simple political or religious stereotyping may have very little to do with the culture as such; for example, the attempt by the Western allies in World War II to influence the attitudes of isolated New Guinea tribes, "The Japanese are bad—kill them"; or the viewing of Protestants as emissaries of Yankee imperialism in remote parts of South America; or a kind of Biblical anti-Semitism among peoples Christianized several centuries ago who have never seen a Jew. But this kind of stereotyping may nevertheless have a great effect on the success of a mission.

This chapter does not concern itself with stereotyping except where it is part of the national character of a given people, as, for example, the way in which repudiation of peasant dialects and the "broken English" spoken by uneducated immigrants in the United States has influenced Americans' ability to learn foreign languages, or the way in which the long history of English-Scottish contact has conditioned the attitudes of the Scots toward other peoples by limiting the question of superiority-inferiority to English-Scottish relationships. It is concerned rather with those aspects of different cultures —either the national culture as a whole, or class, regional, or religious versions of the national culture—which are relevant to cross-cultural situations where definite personnel planning is possible.

One such aspect is concerned with the narrowness or breadth of self-definition within a culture. Consideration of caste, religion, rank, or class may take precedence, on the one hand, over wider self-definition as a human being or as a member of a sex. Or, on the other hand, there may be over-narrow self-definition by occupation (a professor, a physician) or in terms of a specific lineage group (a Cecil, a Campbell, a Lowell). The narrower the individual's self-definition, the more precisely delineated will be the types of contact he will have within bureaucratic structures and with people of other nations.

The contacts of the Polynesian Samoans with Germans, New Zealanders, and Americans provide a good illustration. The Samoans are a people among whom achieved rank is of the greatest importance. High chiefly titles are the property of particular lineages, but they are assigned on the basis of personality. The Germans were able to match their rigid codes of civilian and naval etiquette to the Samoan codes and established a relationship within which even Samoan-German marriages, defined in terms of comparable rank, could survive.

After World War I, Western Samoa became a League of Nations mandate governed by New Zealand. The New Zealand administrators came from an assertively one-class society in which the development of any of the class distinctions characteristic of the mother country are avoided, whether between elder and younger brothers, the better born and more humbly born, the rich and the poor, the educated and the less educated, or those who perform more or less honorific types of work. Among a people with a different culture this egalitarianism might have been a relief and might have produced better cross-cultural relationships. The Samoans, however, classified the New Zealanders' behavior as lacking in style. They found shirt sleeves sloppy after the carefully starched collars of the Germans. The New Zealanders had little respect for the Samoans' insistence on the importance of rank. As a result, cross-cultural relationships deteriorated badly, culminating in the Mau of the late nineteen-twenties and, forty years later, this deterioration is still expressed in the determined separatism of the Western Samoans.

Relationships in Eastern Samoa, which was administered by the United States Navy until after World War II, followed another course. A civilian American administration would almost certainly have run afoul of American racial attitudes and attempted to establish lines of social differentiation along strictly ethnic lines, with intolerance of cross-ethnic marriages and the emergence of a caste-like situation. However, the United States Navy, not unlike other navies of the world, based a large number of fine social distinctions on rank, a situation which the Samoans found completely congenial. Strict protocol could be worked out in kava ceremonies, where each hierarchy honored the other.

Difficulties only arose in those rare instances when an enlisted man who had been promoted to officer rank was unsure of his status, or when a titled Samoan became a clerk in a government department administered by such an officer, or occasionally when enlisted men attempted to establish relationships with Samoan girls from ranking families on the basis of American contempt for all members of another race, regardless of status. Otherwise, cross-cultural relationships were remarkably smooth, and the one small disturbance in the nineteen thirties arose partly from the ambitions of an American girl to become a queen of Samoa by marrying a high-ranking Samoan and working to attain Eastern Samoa's independence.

A similar type of contact occurs in present-day New Guinea when refugee physicians from Eastern and Central Europe are sent to work for the public health department of New Guinea. Men whose picture of their occupational status includes an office in a great European city and the respect accorded a professor of medicine feel demeaned and confused by practicing among half-naked primitive peoples, whom they classify as "lower than the lowest peasants." An extreme callousness results, which is hardly in the tradition of a physician's expected sensitivity to suffering. This situation is confusing not only to the peoples of New Guinea but also to Australian members of the medical services, who take professional pride in the difficulties that must be overcome—the vicissitudes of mountain climbing, operating with inadequate equipment, and the general rigors of a pioneer situation—all of which represent a challenge to the Australian with his pioneer tradition of successful survival on a harsh and difficult continent.

Every detail of self-definition and the varying degrees of its rigidity must be taken into account, since otherwise the most unexpected results may occur. American women are accustomed to dress for public places in ways which will command unabashed attention from strangers. In fact, a type of staring which recognizes their feminine attractiveness is a tribute. When they find themselves surrounded by Arab Moslems who combine staring from a distance with the greatest circumspectness of approach, American women, in their ignorance, feel at the same time safe and flattered. However, the estimate of Western morals, which develops slowly in the mind of the respectfully staring gardener, may have serious international repercussions later on.

Self-definition, then, is one important indicator for cross-cultural work: the narrowness and rigidity of roles; the degree of contrast in expected behavior in roles viewed as similar (behavior appropriate to executives, to women, to physicians, to clerks, etc.); contrasts in the status accorded individuals because of race, sex, or nationality as compared with the status accorded to them because of lineage, education, position, and the like.

Very often a man's social position in his home country is quite different from that which he has within the protocol of a foreign mission, in the administration of a dependent country, or in the narrowly defined hierarchies of limited occasions, such as life on shipboard during a voyage. The British are more accustomed to these contrasts than are Americans, who find it very confusing to shift from high to low status as the situation demands and who respond by a continuous endeavor to stabilize relationships. Their uneasiness often leads to an assertive attempt either to establish a superficially egalitarian ethos—as in the ritual use of first names for everyone, which is most disorienting to persons of many other cultures—or else to an attempt to establish hierarchies which are rigidly resistant to other considerations such as lineage and education.

Different kinds of problems arise when a member of a family of high rank in his own country, especially an Asian or African, enters a profession which is recognized in Europe and

America as being primarily based on education and expertise. Often he will substitute his sense of innate high rank for the criteria of training, experience, and skill used by his European or American colleagues. This may result in totally inappropriate behavior in an executive position where rank is substituted for ability, or in a subordinate position where rank is substituted for willingness to accept direction. Where the sense of innate rank—and I am using this term here to cover all claims to innate superiority or right to certain types of deference because of caste, race, nationality, lineage, etc.—clashes with the requirements of an office, severe conflicts develop within the personality of the individual who has to try to reconcile the two.

The problem is particularly acute when several members of a national group in which rank is sharply distinguished are together in a situation which includes foreigners who are ignorant of the distinctions or, as is often the case, who disapprove of the particular types of distinctions prevailing in that group. So, a Western-educated Asian physician may find himself torn between accepting the appropriate deference from his social inferiors, which his European colleagues would interpret as excessive snobbery, or refusing it and injuring the *amour propre* of his fellow countrymen, who are still dependent on a mutual respect for these social differences. Likewise, English public school graduates may get on perfectly well with a colleague who lacks a public school education until someone from another culture raises the one tabooed subject—the school of the man who did not attend a public school.

In situations of this sort, the attempt to work out a *modus operandi* for people who come from cultures with different systems does more harm than good, especially if status points are expressed in subtle tones of voice rather than in conspicuous forms of protocol. So, for example, Anglo-American relationships were vexed throughout World War II by attempts to equate the unequatable. American officers felt that use of their last names represented distant behavior when the British meant it to establish a formal closeness. Likewise, equating national problems, such as British colonies and American slums, or colonialism in India and the American Negro problem, led to misunderstanding. Differences of this kind, which arise among personnel from different status systems, can be forestalled if the individuals involved are trained to avoid all but the most formal equivalences between the systems of the two cultures.

In summary, three systems of self-definition and hierarchy must be kept in mind:

The culture in which a given individual or group was reared: either it is functioning and must be maintained *in absentia;* or it has changed, as in the case of a refugee or after a social revolution; or it is changing at the moment, as in the case of a Westernized son of a conservative Asian family.

The system of the country in which the group is working, including historical patterns of assigning equivalences of position to foreigners (e.g., the expectation that foreigners will use a particular language, rigorously follow their own code, or accede to the host code in particular respects).

The cultural style, usually derived from specific historical cultural roots, of the particular unit of international work (e.g., a navy, an international oil company, a United Nations technical assistance agricultural mission, a financial advisory group).

This cross-cultural style will be partly determined by the national origins of the type of activity. Thus, United States extension techniques have been influential in establishing the international agricultural mission style: British and Dutch overseas experience led the way in establishing the oil company conventions which survive today through direct imitations or assertive deviation on the part of latecomers. If the culturally derived style of any of these units bears a striking resemblance to one particular culture—French or American or British—as is often the case, this similarity can be a source of confusion. Within the unit, members of the culture whose style is dominant feel deceptively "at home"; they tend to relax their cross-cultural watchfulness and to behave "naturally." In turn, those who are members of other cultures tend to identify with French or American or British behavior the frustrations that are due to personalities or the situation of the unit. In both cases the ability to deal with the bureaucratic style, whatever its origins, as distinct from any particular culture, is diminished.

Specific cross-cultural units derive these culturally dominant styles in a number of ways: from national origins, such as primacy in a particular field; from direct cross-cultural modeling, as when the Japanese Navy learned from the Dutch or when Thais were trained in Denmark; from ideology, particular institutions being seen as more characteristic of Western democracy, communism, Asian neutralism, or newly founded independent nations; and from locations, with the culture of the maintenance and clerical staff and the style of communications and transportation exerting a continuous influence (e.g., UNESCO in Paris, FAO in Rome, WHO in Geneva).

Since there is no reason to believe that cultural styles will not persist indefinitely, they must be taken into account in assaying the suitability of a given individual for a given task and in the training and briefing for assignment to a specific unit. An urban-reared economist might fit very well into a financial advisory unit, where personal contacts would be almost entirely limited to high-level contacts with bankers sophisticated in international monetary practice, but he would be less able to administer an agricultural assistance unit with an emphasis on people-to-people contact.

Once the variables that relate to self-definition in the culture of origin, culture of work, and cultural style of working unit have been identified, a number of other problems can be tackled. Although attempts to establish exact equivalences are dangerous and must be avoided, there are wide areas of commonality which can be examined—as, for example, the position of women or religious affiliation. Cultures can be categorized roughly according to the amount of freedom and autonomy given women; to circumvent difficulties, female personnel should not be sent to countries where women have low status, nor should men from such countries be placed in positions where they must show deference to women.

In matters of religion it may sometimes be wiser to ignore the apparent commonality. European Catholics sometimes find it very difficult to work with American Catholics; but their expectation of sharing a common point of view with Protestants may be less, and thus, their disappointments and frustrations may also be fewer working with Protestants than with Catholics. In missions to Israel, Jews from other nations find that they are subject to pressures from which their Gentile teammates are free. In areas where there is tension between two evenly balanced religious groups, someone owing allegiance to neither group may have an easier time.

In general, it is important to make each set of national cultural characteristics explicit and not to take refuge in cross-cultural categories of common occupation or religion. Under such circumstances the appearance of successful contact merely blurs the national cultural differences that exist and only too often exacerbates these differences. This situation is illustrated by the intolerance displayed by American Negro troops in World War I toward members of their own race who spoke French instead of English. Similar misunderstandings occur when European physicians with a broad liberal arts tradition find American physicians uncultured or when university-educated Europeans find themselves at a loss with many Americans who have graduated from state universities.

Another set of dimensions which lends itself to abstraction concerns symmetrical and complementary types of behaviors and the different styles of reciprocity practiced in different cultures. Thus, there are complementary styles where behavior A evokes behavior B (e.g., dominance and submission); symmetrical styles in which behavior A evokes behavior A; and styles where A evokes B, followed by a reversal where the individual or group that displayed B now displays A, which evokes B, as in gift-giving, reversals of host-guest positions, and the like. Most complex societies use all three styles of behavior but with varying meanings.

The overall cultural style can be described in terms of the prevailing relationships between parents and children. A number of contrasts are involved here, since children are always smaller and weaker and dependent on adults for care. So for any culture we find:

Parents	*Children*
Succoring	Dependent
Stronger	Weaker

However, there will be wide variations in the patterns of other attitudes of dominance-submission, exhibitionism-spectatorship, elevation-support, patronage-deference, initiative-response, and so on.

The underlying assumption that initiative always comes from strength in Britain and from weakness in the United States has profound repercussion in international negotiation. The British are often able to regard a 5 percent victory as a successful compromise because they consider this a virtue exercised by the strong. Americans, on the other hand, may regard a 95 percent victory as a defeat because the only possible position for the weaker party is 100 percent uncompromisingness.

Russia provides a third way of handling spectatorship positions, for in Russia spectatorship-exhibitionism appears on both sides of the relationship, with a speaker joining in the applause of his own speech. This mutual mirroring behavior often precludes any accomplishment by a pair, so that the preferred pattern is the *troika,* or working unit composed of three. Or in negotiations with the Japanese, the preference for the actual leader to remain in the background, a dissociation of power from the center of the stage, can give rise to problems for those unaware of this pattern.

Compared to relationships with a fundamental asymmetry, which can be either exaggerated or compensated for, peer relationships are basically symmetrical in character, but the forms of symmetry may vary. Men of equal status may treat each other with great distance, reserving warmth and intimacy for asymmetrical relationships that involve differences in status. Or, on the other hand, peer relationships may be the only ones in which intimacy and ease are permitted. Peer relationships between males in the United States are basically distant; jollity, ceremonial competitiveness, roughhousing, and the jocular insult are used to maintain this distance. Coming from a culture where the peer relationship, especially in youth, was warm and intimate, Germans find it difficult to "form friendships" with Americans. In international work both hierarchical and peer relationships will be affected by the expectations and manners that accompany them in different cultures.

Reciprocal relationships, in which an individual alternates as host and guest or as giver and receiver of gifts or favors, while easier to formulate, also cause friction, especially between Asians and Europeans. In such a reciprocal relationship it is possible to hold the advantage by always being in the donor position, always one up on the other person; or a relationship may be intensified by the failure to complete the sequence with a return gift or favor; or again a desperate attempt may be made to achieve absolute equality by exact matching or by efforts to liquidate an obligation as quickly as possible. When the individual of one culture is primarily anxious about how his gift has been received and appreciated and the individual from the other culture believes that the subtlest form of gratitude is to delay any acknowledgment, "not discharging the obligation too quickly," the possibilities for misunderstanding are obvious.

In cross-cultural situations the host-guest positions are sometimes fixed for long periods, or equivalence in gift exchange may be virtually impossible to achieve. Lack of flexibility in a relationship where flexibility is essential leads to accusations of "strings attached," "ingratitude," or "trying to make a good thing of it." What is necessary here is clear recognition that paired relationships such as host-guest, superior-subordinate, native-foreigner, can be as asymmetrical as parent-child relationships are. The realities of the situation transcend particular cultural interpretations and only by making these interpretations explicit will the cultural differences become manageable. Thus, a guest may be seen as dependent and in need of protection, as exploitive and a burden, as an investment in future favors or protection, as someone who honors one's house (or, on the contrary, someone who violates the privacy of one's home), and in each of these different contexts the position of the host must be reciprocally viewed by the guests. The same approach holds for many other fixed relationships in which the cross-cultural worker is involved: subordinate-superior, national versus international agency, business versus government, government versus voluntary agency, among others. If the fixed asymmetry is recognized, the cultural differences can be made conscious and objective, hence manageable.

Recognizing the importance of these differences enables us to determine the fitness or unfitness of members of specific cultures to engage in particular kinds of cross-cultural work. When the members of a culture have been minority group traders for long periods of time, such as the Syrians, special accommodation skills may have been developed which make it possible for them to fit in among strangers without any essential loss of identity. In fact, this fitting in is part of their identity. The Dutch over many generations developed the ability to live overseas for long periods while maintaining the sense of their own identity and planning their lives in the expectation of one day returning to the Netherlands to live. In this connection, immigration, which means severing all ties with the mother country, has proved very difficult for the Dutch. The Scots, with a stabilized attitude toward the politically dominant English, are particularly successful in the United States, where different attitudes toward the English prevail. They also work well in situations involving racial tensions. Wherever they go, the French carry with them a sense of form and style. When they can see their role as the introducers of form into situations that were hitherto amorphous, they become happily engrossed in their mission.

If two societies have both incorporated into their sense of national identity an element like size or independence in the face of great odds, then a kind of cultural sympathy may be established, as between Denmark and Thailand. Sometimes a tradition of past warfare between two groups provides a basis for the acceptance of one when the other is rejected, as, for example, the greater acceptability of Americans in British colonial areas. Building on such hostilities is always risky, however, for those who welcome Americans because they are not British or British because they are not Dutch will combine with their welcome a sense of guilt toward their colonial past. There is likely to be covert insistence that the British or Dutch really were more cultured or did things better and this complicates their acceptance of aid overtly welcomed.

On the whole it is safer to build on positive rather than on negative traits and historical situations: on the basis of an old friendship between one country and another or because the members of one culture display traits which the members of another culture presently wish to emulate. This is often a matter of timing. American casualness about manual labor may compromise the acceptability of Americans in a particular area until ideas of democracy and equality become desirable. Then this same lack of ceremony and willingness to use one's hands become models for young people who are anxious to imitate the ways of the West. Distinctions can also be made between types of initial ease and friendliness in different cultures and the rate at which relationships are established or work gets under way in a given cross-cultural situation. The Americans' ease of first contact is a positive value here, but their impatience and inability to wait gracefully are handicaps.

Sheerly temperamental qualities—in the sense that, in a given culture, certain elements of innate temperament are institutionalized—can be very important. An illustration is the ability of Spaniards to work among Arabs. The two groups have certain unanalyzed affinities, some but not all of which are historical in their origins. Physical size may also be a significant factor. The very large Dutch official working with the slightly built Indonesians had a precedent in the friendly giants of the Indonesian shadow plays. It was a different matter, however, when on state occasions the ceremonial included wives. For while the Dutch official had a diminutive fairy tale princess at his side, the slender rajah had to convoy a Dutch matron of—to him—truly alarming proportions. The effect on Japanese-American relationships of sheer size differentials has been studied with revealing results.

While it would take a very extensive research project to work out all the relevant variables, such matters as relative size, the position of women, the degree of deference to age, a preference for oratory and flowery language, the speed of interaction, a preference for frankness versus circumlocution, the need for elaborate face-saving devices, etc., can be kept in mind. By careful interviewing of experienced foreign personnel it should be possible to establish workable indicators of which countries are most likely to contribute people who will be successful in which other countries and in what types of situations. The very simplest indicators should be used first. For example, where there is a great difference in height, it is safer to put members of such cultures together in situations where they will be seated most of the time.

Third-culture positions

So far a great deal of attention has been given to the fit between members of two cultures. In a task involving relations between two cultures which contain elements of dominance, exploitation, conquest, racial superiority, or antagonistic egalitarianisms, probably the most effective cross-cultural technique is to assign the project to an individual from a third culture which is not closely identified with either of the other two. Not only can he view the cultural behavior of the others with greater clarity, but he must also make an effort to learn something of both cultures: for example, traditional Netherland legal practice and contemporary Indonesian legal practice in Indonesia; or traditional Spanish and later American and contemporary Philippine legal practice in the Philippines.

In the latter case a Spaniard might overestimate Spanish survivals and an American might regard present-day practice as a deteriorated version of American practice, but an Englishman or a German would have to look at the matter afresh.

Language is particularly significant in this third culture context. Where the first or even the second language of a country has a European base—as Spanish in Mexico, French in Canada, English in the Philippines or, more remotely, Creole in Haiti, English in the British West Indies, and Neo-Melanesian in New Guinea—someone who speaks the European language as a mother tongue will inevitably regard the local tongue as deteriorated or, at best, archaic. Although he may have been chosen for the post because he spoke Spanish, or French, or English, learning to speak a patois is not easy for a cultivated adult, and in most instances he will never learn to speak it well. So, in some parts of New Guinea there were administrators who as speakers of English found it more congenial to learn a native lingua franca, Motuan, but in that part of New Guinea administered by the Germans, pidgin English (now called Neo-Melanesian) became a real language which the Germans helped to codify and preserve. The current ferment over preservation of languages of world scope as opposed to a patriotic emphasis on local languages is likely to increase the sensitivity of civil servants to the way in which their local version of a world language is treated. In such circumstances the man who speaks French well as a *second language* will be able to play a special role in working with French Canadians, Haitians, or Cambodians, or in French-speaking African countries.

Here again a cultural factor can be noted because such expert speakers of a second language often come from small countries like Switzerland, the Scandinavian countries, or the Netherlands. For these peoples, learning other languages involves recognition of the fact that one's own culture is one among many, an attitude that is especially valuable in cross-cultural work. While cross-cultural marriage may also lead to proficiency in using a second language and understanding the accompanying cultural attitudes, a third culture position which is based on an emotional relationship like marriage is less likely to produce balanced, predictable behavior. It is probably more useful to be a member of a culture or of a group in a society which has a tradition of cultural pride in the ability to understand foreign customs and to deal with foreigners. It must be expected, however, that cross-cultural marriages will continue to provide many of those persons interested in and willing to work in cross-cultural fields, either in the first or second generation.

Cross-national love affairs and antipathies

If an individual is to work successfully for any length of time among people of another culture, it is essential that he respect them. Furthermore, it is desirable that he like them rather than dislike them, but it is almost equally desirable that, however he may respond selectively to particular individuals, he feel neither intense love nor intense hate for the people as a group. (The ability to like or dislike the individual members of another culture with the same discrimination that would be displayed in one's own culture is one of the surest signs that one understands the culture and that no irrational, stereotyped prejudices, either positive or negative, are interfering with a free flow of cross-cultural communication.)

Excessive identification clouds discrimination, both in terms of one's own culture and in terms of the culture onto which certain intense attitudes are projected. In European countries as well as in some non-European countries, certain other nations have been selected for romantic idealization by poets and song makers, painters and writers. This artistic treatment provides the cultural matrix for an international, undiscriminating attachment. Thus, the English child who reads *Kim* or D. H. Lawrence's stories of Italy; the "greenery yallery foot in the gallery Grosvenor Square young man" reading about Japan, and his Japanese counterpart dreaming about Baudelaire; the Chilean seeing France as the source of all literary and artistic culture; the Indonesian who dreamed of going overseas to

Holland; and the native-born Australian who still calls England "home"—all of these culturally fostered daydreams carry with them motivation for cross-cultural work.

But they also carry dangers, the greater perhaps because they have been given weight and authority by the work of great writers. It is just such writing about another country which the man assigned to that country is most likely to read; yet it is not the best preparation for his task. An American going to England or to the Netherlands for the first time could learn a great deal from reading "The English: Are They Human?" by a Netherlander, but a Netherlander on his way to England would only have his long-existing prejudices confirmed.

Long-standing cross-cultural antipathies, false identification, or ignorance may be equally obfuscating. An American reared on *Mother India* is even worse prepared for work in modern India than is an Englishman reared exclusively on Kipling. Or we may contrast the attitudes toward Greece held by educated prerevolutionary Russians and Englishmen of the same period. To the Russian, Italy represented the classical tradition and Greece a primitive Christian tradition, while the Englishman often identified Italy with Catholicism whereas, for him, Greece represented the highest flowering of the human spirit. The more highly educated and the more sophisticated the person chosen for cross-cultural work, the more he will be subject to these deeply entrenched attitudes. If these attitudes are directly involved, either through conscious choice of a country about which a great deal is already known or by purposeful cultivation of this type of knowledge, relationships with the present-day inhabitants of the nation may be distorted and unsatisfactory.

Equally vexing but quite different problems face those of limited education and narrow social background who find themselves working in another culture, especially persons who come from the group which, in the United States and Great Britain, is technically called the "lower middle class" and which corresponds roughly to the "petite bourgeoisie" of

Western Europe. Members of this group have a tendency to convert the smallest behaviors, food habits, posture, gesture, or niceties of speech into matters of morality. Eating with a knife, shaking hands or not shaking hands, washing or not washing the hands on stated occasions, mentioning "certain subjects"—all are given tremendous weight. One who has had a cosmopolitan training combining historical depth and travel can recognize that other manners are as complex as his own, but this is not so easy for those from a more restricted background. Differences in food, in hygiene, in dress are shocking, and the shock is hard to moderate. Initiation into foreign habits by slow degrees, letting each shock wear off, can be more effective than asking these people to make the transformations which are possible for the cosmopolitan—between a dinner in Buckingham Palace and a feast given by a desert sheik.

Second-level cultural learning

We have been dealing almost exclusively with particular cultures and with the ways a member of one of these cultures reacts to members of certain other cultures. However, in almost all types of cultural work today, it is seldom possible for an individual to work continuously in a particular area of the world. What is needed, therefore, is not so much a means of evaluating how an Englishman will fit in Venezuela or a Brazilian in Indonesia. More important is a method for recognizing an already developed, incipient cross-cultural sensitivity which will make an individual readily adaptable to many different cultures as represented by individuals, bureaucratic styles, or whole populations.

Here again cultural factors are involved. Examples are: coming from a small country that is proud to be a small country; coming from a new country that is proud to be a new country; coming from a minority group that is proud of its long, successful maintenance of minority status (Scots, Armenians, Lebanese); coming from a country with a strong occupational emphasis on out-of-country activities (seafaring, banking, trade). Even though such activities may embody elements of patronage and superiority, they nevertheless carry a cultural message that other people are different, that they have other ways and other languages, and that it is possible to get to know them, learn their languages, and understand their customs. The most valuable heritage for those entering cross-cultural work, then, is not one of specific attitudes and knowledge about particular cultures as such, but rather one in which accidents of birth and education, regional and occupational affiliation permit an expectation of cross-cultural understanding.

In most countries there are sections, classes, regions, occupations in which the opposite attitude is taught; where the ways of all foreigners are despised, foreigners are feared, and all foreign languages are regarded as heathenish. When individuals who come from such backgrounds decide to engage in cross-cultural work, their choice may be seen as a repudiation of the narrowness of their home environment. Their reactions may have great intensity, as when the boy from the heart of a continent who longs to go to sea recites:

Bred as we among the mountains,
Can the Sailor understand?
The divine exhilaration
Of the first League out from land.

These individuals have their counterparts in those who are reared abroad and who dream with passionate intensity of a very much idealized home or home culture. They provide many of the idealists in cross-cultural work. Such persons can be used but not purposefully cultivated. It will be well to concentrate in selecting people for cross-cultural work on those attitudes of hospitality to other cultures which are based on expectation of difference rather than a repudiation of a narrow home environment. In race relations it is the formerly strongly prejudiced person who becomes the zealot. The man who has grown up in a culture where all races were treated as members of the same human race will be a reliable, steady worker. Thus, the positive valuation of difference based on cultural experiences is the most reliable index of success for cross-cultural work.

When we wrote *Balinese Character* (Bateson, G., and Mead, 1942), Bateson and I combined Erik Erikson's zonal-modal analysis (Erikson, 1963), which I had worked on since 1934 and Bateson since 1939, with the ideas of symmetrical and complementary relationships. The zonal relationships were all complementary, while whole body relationships tended to be symmetrical, the inclusion of objects making them reciprocal. This can be further elaborated so that all relationships that involve males, and thus genitals designed for intrusion, tend to be complementary in character, whereas if the emphasis is upon the female as lacking intrusive genitals, relationships between females tend to be symmetrical. Anality, involving substances as a mode, regularly involves reciprocity.

I believe that one test of the usefulness of any formulation is the extent to which it can be transferred into other useful formulations, based on different data. *Balinese Character,* in which we used Erikson's categories, is one example of such transformation operations. Sophisticated somatotyping, in which the emphasis is upon the relationship among types within any given population and not upon absolute proportions, may be expected to give another set of transforms, as presaged in the chapter on types in *Naven* (Bateson, G., 1936b). The essential underlying theme of all of these analyses is the link between the biologically or situationally given and the ways in which this given is elaborated upon within a total cultural setting.

Male and Female Contrasts

In 1943, while she was working on a war-relevant memorandum on Thailand—as one of the first studies of culture at a distance—Ruth Benedict wrote a description of the relationships between Thai men and women.

MALE DOMINANCE IN THAI CULTURE

The most revealing of all Thai summaries of male and female character is the proverb which is on every tongue: "Man is paddy; woman is rice"; i.e., man is the seed rice able to reproduce itself, woman is rice polished for eating. As Thai women informants said, "She can only be swallowed once," "she can't reproduce unless a man comes to her." But a man "can produce by himself." An informant illustrated with a "rice" (woman) as a kernel inside a closed circle; of "paddy" (man) as a short straight line with arrows radiating out from him. The proverb is used in the education of girls to teach them to guard their virtue—for they can only be "eaten" once; i.e., by one man. In the education of boys, it bears testimony to their superiority; they are the "seed" which produces the harvest.

In spite of all the freedom of Thai village women and of the wives of officials, the one superiority—fertility—which is ascribed to them by most peoples is not theirs by Thai definition. They provide a nest for the child in the womb and nourish their husbands, but they have not the virtue of creativity in themselves.

Yet they can nourish their husbands well. As men say in Thailand, "A play friend is not equal to a die friend and a boy friend is not equal to a girl friend," i.e., a man is a fair-weather friend, but from a woman one can expect loyalty till death. When a man courts a girl, he selects one to whom, in the Thai phrase, "he can trust his life in sickness and his obsequies after death." It is the woman—not the husband, as in our Episcopal marriage service—who must "cherish . . . till death do us part."

This is the great Thai daydream, and it is the betrayal of this daydream that is usually elaborated in story and proverb and simile. A woman who does not satisfy this dream, since she has no other justification in living, has betrayed her kind. The Thai say: "A male elephant, a crocodile, and a loving wife, put not your trust in these." They say: "Three days' absence from home and your wife is another's."

The best statement of what men hope and fear for in their wives is the writing of the Siamese philosopher quoted by Young (1900; pp. 86–88).

> 1. Some wives are to their husbands as a younger sister. They look to their husbands for approving smiles as the reward of their kind and affectionate forethought. They confide in him and feel tenderly toward him. And when they have once discovered the wish, the taste, and the ideas of him whose approval they respect, they devote themselves thoughtfully and assiduously to the realization of his desires. Their own impulsive passions and temper are kept under strict control lest some hasty word should mar the harmony of their union.
>
> 2. Some wives are to their husbands as an elder sister. They watch sedulously their husband's outgoings and incomings so as to prevent all occasion for scandal. They are careful as to the condition of his wardrobe and keep it always in order for every occasion. They are diligent in preserving from the public gaze anything that might impair the dignity of their family. When their lord and master is found wanting in any particular, they neither fret nor scold, but wait patiently for the time when they can best effect a reformation in his morals and lead him toward the goal of upright manly conduct.
>
> 3. Some wives are to their husbands like a mother. They are ever seeking for some good thing that may bring gladness to the heart of the man for whom they live. They desire him to be excellent in every particular, and will themselves make

any sacrifice to secure their object. When sorrow or trouble overtakes them, they hide it away from the eyes of him they love. All their thoughts center round him, and they so order their conversation and actions that in themselves he may find a worthy model for imitation. Should he fall sick, they tend him with unfailing care and patience.

4. Some wives are to their husbands as a common friend (i.e., "play friend"). They desire to stand on an exactly equal footing with him (i.e., they give tit for tat). If ill-nature is a feature in the character of their husbands, they cultivate the same fault in themselves. They will quarrel with him on the slightest provocation. They meet all his suggestions with an excess of carping criticism. They are always on the lookout for any infringement of what they deem their rights, and should the husband desire them to perform any little service for him, he must approach the subject with becoming deference or their refusal is instant and absolute.

5. Some wives wish to rule their husbands. Their language and manners are of a domineering nature. They treat the man as if he were a slave, scolding, commanding, and forbidding with unbecoming asperity. The husbands of such women are a miserable cringing set of men.

6. Some wives are of the robber kind. Their only idea in getting married is the possession of a slave and the command of the purse. If there is money in the purse, they are never satisfied until they have it in their own grasp. Such wives generally take to gambling and staking money in the lottery, or purchasing useless articles. They have no care as to where the money comes from or by whose labors it is earned, so long as they can gratify their own extravagant and ruinous fancies.

7. Some wives are of the murderous kind and possess revengeful tempers. Being malicious and fault-finding, they never appreciate their own homes and families, and are always seeking for sympathies from outside. They share their secrets with other men, using their pretended domestic discomfort as a cloak for their own vice and an excuse for their greatest misdeeds.

The wives who are on a female pattern are all "good"; they are "younger sister," "elder sister," and "mother." They will be "die friends," and in looking for a wife a man looks for one who will reproduce his relations with the women of his family. Yet Thai men are so rarely impotent that it is not a subject of gossip, not even a cursing accusation. These wives who follow the pattern of their husband's mothers and sisters are submissive and ideal.

The wives who take their prototype from males are "bad." From the whole context and from the whole description of Thai concepts and behavior in this memorandum, this is evidently not because of taboos separating the respective spheres of the sexes but is, rather, a projection upon women of all the non-hierarchal relations between men. These latter are relatively "difficult" in Thailand. First there is the "play friend" type who returns evil for evil and will do her husband no "little service" unless he pretends deference. Then there is the domineering woman who orders her husband about, and he becomes a "miserable cringing" being. The "robber kind" are out for money and interested only in spending it at their whim. Only the last and "murderous kind" betray their husbands by taking lovers. Wandering sexual fancy is only characteristic of one out of four "bad" wifely types which disturbs a man's peace.

The man's attitude toward the relations of the sexes is given symbolic elaboration in the national game of kite-flying—which is played exclusively by men. This game is carried out with a skill which all observers have admired. It is a "courtship" of a female kite and a male kite. The female kite is a four-sided diamond shape and goes up with a lilting motion to the accompaniment, in any exhibition game, of a dancing tune from the orchestra. There is a special orchestra for the female kite and another for the male kite when it finally comes up to "court" the female. The man who flies the female kite stays in one part of the field, and his kite is not allowed to cruise. Presently another kite-flyer from another end of the field sends up his male kite. This is a much heavier kite, perhaps six times as big, in the shape of a five-pointed star. It ascends higher than the female kite and cruises toward the female to "capture" it. It must not get too close to the body of the little kite or its balance would be upset, and it would "lose"; then the male kite's orchestra would play a lamenting tune and if the female kite has an orchestra, it will play triumphantly. But the string of the male kite has attached to it, up toward the kite, two small curved twigs of bamboo which project out in four points. The female kite has a slacker cord attached to its string up in the air, and into this loop the male kite must get its tentacles. It swoops down on the dancing female kite and, if it is successful, drags her in triumph to its end of the field where they both fly entangled to the triumphant music of the male kite's orchestra. She is "his."

The male is the huge, heavy kite, the female the little, dancing one. The male is the cruiser, the female is anchored. The male pulls her into his orbit and flies with her in triumph; if he gets too close to her and falls, it is "she" who caused his fall, and "she" triumphs. "I have never, I think, seen the Siamese so serious, with attention so riveted, as when they assemble in thousands every afternoon for hours at a stretch to fly their kites. That for them is the real business of life" (Campbell, 1902, p. 107).

The game well symbolizes the relation of men and women. Men are not doubtful of their masculinity—which is here symbolized in the kite's size and shape and activity. Men mark their kites with their insignia or name and may have three or four at hand to continue the game if one falls or is damaged. The object of the game is to keep a "wife" within their orbit and both male and female "flying"; if "he" falls, it is the woman's fault, and "she" has won. But attacking her too closely—perhaps it would be fair to say dominating her, or possessing her, in the European sense—would mean, in the kite game, falling to the ground and being defeated. Thai men assume that she is small and fragile and has no "game" to play unless a man "captures" her. It is the same statement under another simile which they make in "Woman is rice, but man is paddy." Success, for the man, depends upon skilled maneuvering and a not too close approach to the body of the other kite—on one's own wits, in daily life, and one's canny skepticism about others.

The plots of their impromptu "sings" show the rules of the game between men and women as they are thought to work themselves out in Thai behavior. After the male leader has sung the invocation, the answering female leader invokes dead women leaders to assist her "in making men humble and discomfited, in fact to make her victory over them absolutely crushing." It is again the "contest" of the kite game. The most popular ways in which the "sing" may develop is "contending for a lady" or contending for a man. In the first form, described by Prince Bidyalankarana (1926), the husband is urging his wife to return to him no matter what her infidelities; "despite her faithlessness his love for her is as deep as ever, and he implores her to abandon her lover and return home to husband and child." It is not necessary for the husband to defend his "honor"; he wants her within his orbit. In the plot of contending for a man, the man finds himself "an unhappy fellow who stands between two sharp tongues." He has lost the initiative to the women, and the story only ends when he is once more paired with one of them. Obviously, the "crushing victory" for which the women ask is pre-eminence in repartee; they do not seek a "defeat" of men in the sense of humiliating them.

The high place of the male in his world is powerfully reinforced in real life by Buddhist teachings and by the male prerogative of the monkhood, from which women are unconditionally excluded. But the Buddhist doctrine of man's superiority is divorced from sex; by definition the monk is asexual. Among the Thai this operates merely to remove from men a possible source of anxiety; they do not have to prove their virility by affairs with women or even by their relations with their wives. They are, in Pallegoix's words, "almost passionless"—and one man in twenty is at any given time unquestionably chaste, since he is in a monastery—yet impotence is hardly recognized except that it is admitted that it might be found in a psychopath. King Mongkut retired to a monastery for more than twenty years, and when he came out, at forty-five, he fathered more than eighty children. This is regarded as natural, and the enforced celibacy of the monk is regarded as equally unneeding of remark; it is not considered as a serious frustration. Even today reformers speak of the harm not eating after midday may do to a delicate constitution, but they do not speak of sex frustration.

The villagers, especially in later life, enjoy bandying insults and they have a language for this which is obscene in their sense. It accuses the other person of sexual irregularities, even of incest. This is what is referred to when they speak of "the mouth of a market woman," but the older men take active part also. The more usual form of insult, however, is a delicate manipulation of respect terms and gestures; the least shade of difference carries the insult. (Benedict, 1952)

There remained, however, a thorough application of the ideas of symmetry, complementarity, and reciprocity to the way in which sex roles and the attitudes between the sexes are culturally stylized, and the extent to which there is a biological basis for any differences that recur.

In 1949, when I wrote *Male and Female* (Mead, 1949), I added to previous discussions of sex and temperament a further treatment of reciprocity, the third mode that had been least dealt with in *Naven*. The Manus of the Admiralty Islands of New Guinea represented a perfect example of reciprocal relationships between men and women, and parents and children, from the way in which the child treated his mother's breast as a piece of rubber tubing through which a substance passed, to the statement of all human relationships—brother and sister, husband and wife—as an exchange of tangible services.

It was possible at that time to identify a few apparent universals, using existing materials from the seven Pacific Island cultures in which I had worked, although whether these universals were to be attributed to biological sex differences, or to the elaboration of the experiential circumstance that women bore and reared children, was and is not yet clear. It could be said, however, that tasks that required greater strength, distance, and risk were universally assigned to men, and that whatever the tasks assigned, those performed by men were accorded greater prestige than the same tasks performed by women (Mead, 1974b, 1975). I placed considerable emphasis on the contrasts between child and adult bodies and upon the saliency of childbearing in cultures where people wore little clothing and male constructions were not overwhelmingly large, so that womb envy and its ceremonial elaboration was widespread. In the light of our present-day knowledge, these still appear to be universals, although always relative—the largest animals, whichever they are, will be assigned to men; the greatest distances, however short these may be, will still be the appropriate journey for men. But beyond these, there are enormous varieties in which end linkages can be set up:

MEN	WOMEN
shedders of blood	forbidden to shed blood
pure because undefiled by menstruation and childbearing	defiled
or unable to discharge bad blood naturally	able to rid themselves of bad blood naturally

MEN	WOMEN
risk their lives heroically in war	risk their lives heroically in childbearing
able to make yams grow	antithetical to yams because of impurity of blood
	or vulnerable to yams because of childbearing functions

MEN	WOMEN
bigger, stronger, able to travel farther	smaller, weaker, homebound
deal with large animals	deal with plants, insects, shellfish
hunt and kill	deal with animals after they are killed
manage the fastest form of transportation	allowed least rapid form of transportation
able to deal with machines which are successors of large animals	unable to deal with machines
	or able to deal with electronic programming, provided they remain invisible (a privilege accorded the obese, the visibly handicapped, and members of minority groups)

MEN	WOMEN
vastly fertile, able to father innumerable offspring	only able to shelter offspring provided by male
or neutral, contributing little to the ongoingness of life	or symbols of fertility, productive of children, harvests, sources of life and of food

MEN	WOMEN
able to perform magic by virtue of artificial knowledge	witches by inheritance of pacts with evil spirits

MEN	WOMEN
the sun	the moon
the day	the night
the right hand	the left hand

(These are universals which can be distorted as in the Stalinist revisions of old Russian folklore wherein the Czar as the sun and Czarina as the moon were replaced by Stalin, sun in one hand and moon in the other, standing on the earth to give birth to a collective farm (Mead, 1951; Hoyt, 1949).

MEN	WOMEN
(Tiger, 1969) bonded, cooperative, political	unbonded, individually tied to offspring, apolitical

MEN	WOMEN
producers	users, consumers, preservers, distributors

There are also the assignments to men or women of characteristics that are basically matters of temperament, such as bravery, possessiveness, activity, passivity, initiative, responsiveness, and a great variety of other traits that may either be recognized as characteristic of both men and women, or attributed to only one sex, class, or caste. Historically the male role in paternity must have been unknown for countless thousands of years; its discovery (Murray, 1963) must have been made by women, who were the only ones in a position to make it. It is tempting to regard planting of seeds as a feminine discovery and a feminine imagery, while hunting and herding provided a knowledge of the male as sire of many offspring. But the Thai material is a vivid illustration of how the imagery of plants, seemingly more appropriate for the stylization of women, may be taken over by men.

It may well be that we have to look not to intrinsic male and female traits but to a constellation in which those who bear children must be protected from activities that will interfere with that role, that is, excessive mobility, absence from home and offspring, isolation from help by others during childbearing, and any requirement of killing living things that conflicts with a basic requirement of nourishing a new and fragile life Métraux, 1975). In complementary fashion, those who do not bear children must be free to range widely in search of food, to fight to protect females and the young, and to mold and shape the environment to provide better for women and children. We would then construct the following diagram:

MEN	WOMEN
free ranging	homebound
protective	needing protection
willing to risk lives and kill in defense of women and children	forbidden to kill
innovative in making environmental changes, building, conquering, inventing	receptive and adaptive within the artificialities created by men
achievers	lifegivers

It would still be possible to point to the endocrines as adapting men and women to differentially active roles, and even to posit some differences in brain function, possibly located in the retillian brain, as very deep learned behavior (Maclean, 1974). And it would still be possible to recognize that men, deprived of their role of protectors, might develop pathologies, that women deprived of the role of lifegivers might develop pathologies, and the societies that distort these mutually complementary and reinforcing roles might also suffer certain pathologies (Mead, 1975b).

But the real use of an end linkage type of analysis comes into play when we attribute strength or superiority of any sort to one sex and then associate any activity also assigned to one sex as either important or negligible, compatible with strength or weakness. So caring for the individual, the child, and the old has been assigned to women, and the professional elaboration of these roles, in teaching small children, nursing, and care and provision of food, have also been assigned to women. Thus the professions of nursing, teaching small children, dealing with nutrition or home management became demeaning to men. Similarly, giving a woman the role of engineer, driver, or welder, putting her in the armed services, letting her be a veterinarian dealing with large animals, permitting her to drive the largest and most powerful engines around, whether these be trucks, airplanes, or space capsules is seen as altering the necessary proportions in the relationship between the activities of men and women.

An end linkage analysis would always make it possible to suggest caution in the assignment of any task specifically to one sex or the other. If assigned to women, men may reject it, or despise men who accept it; if assigned to men, women may hesitate to attempt it, or be punished by men and other women if they do. It should also be possible to make an estimate of which roles seem irrevocably attached to one sex or the other, and how many roles can be effectively dissociated from any form of sex typing. The linkage of some roles, like the protection of life and the protection from taking life, to women, and the demand for an aggressively protective role that includes a willingness to risk life, to men, may be found to be essential to the preservation of society within which children are reared safely to adulthood. But conversely, it may be found that any society that associates some easily shareable skill or role with only one sex imposes suffering on both sexes in the form of the denial of education, limitations on playing particular musical instruments, or partaking in certain performing professions, shopping, or decision making in political matters. So the assignment by sex of any activity that is not intimately related to the maintenance of a dynamic equilibrium between men and women in the interests of children and the survival of society may be destructive, but failure to maintain the basic minimum may be destructive also.

It may well be, however, that instead of the diffusion of sex roles and the possible denial of real differences with disastrous effects, we may move from the dyadic assignment of roles to the assignment of individuals of both sexes who are exempted from the roles required by the exigencies of rearing and educating children. For such a proportion of the population, the attribution of any sex-associated characteristics might vanish, and a large proportion of individuals be allowed simply to be human beings in an overpopulated world who have bypassed the role of parent and chosen instead to contribute to human culture as individuals.

Thus even a superficial look at end linkage analyses in which the associated and assigned roles deny biological givens is sufficient to provide a warning. All parents are bigger and stronger than all little children. When this is denied, when the parent pretends to be unable to control a willful two-year-old, or to save it from deadly danger, then a perversion occurs that may produce great insecurity in both parent and child. If women as mothers do need protection, the denial of that protection for the possible reason that women work for money produces the kind of terrible distortion that is found in present-day America, where nine million fatherless households are headed by women who are paid less—because earning more money is a male prerogative—but deserted because their ability to earn some money exempts males from the kind of protectiveness that was historically demanded of them. Fathers are always the same sex as their little boys and are therefore better mentors in male skills, such as the control and appropriate use of aggression, than are mothers, who are themselves unable to practice what they can only preach. The assignment to children of too much responsibility and choice overburdens them in the face of the obvious reality that their parents are, or should be, able to take that responsibility. At the same time, the continuous observation of the way end linkages are organized in contrasts between parents and children, and men and women alerts to change; it was undoubtedly a major factor in my discernment of the kind of generation break that occurred after World War II, when the assumptions of shared experience between parents and their children could no longer be made, and parents could no longer provide models for the future, nor could they expect their children ever to follow in their footsteps (Mead, 1970).*

As Gregory Bateson's continuing, consistent, and penetrating search continues, those of us who work with him, either as individuals or in groups, are illuminated in our own searches, and given threads to follow, far from those he has chosen, only to return again to find new threads, to hold in newly instructed hands.

* The most recent application of the model has been a paper by Deborah Gewertz (in press), given at the American Anthropological Association in 1976.

NOTES

Bateson, Gregory, "Social Structure of the Iatmul People of the Sepik River," *Oceania* 2 (1932): 245–91.

———, "Ritual Transvesticism on the Sepik River, New Guinea," *International Congress of Anthropological and Ethnological Sciences,* first session (London: Royal Anthropological Institure, 1934), pp. 274–75.

———, *Naven* (Cambridge: Cambridge Univ. Press, 1936).

———, "The Preferred Types," *Naven* (Cambridge: Cambridge Univ. Press, 1936), pp. 160–70.

———, "Morale and National Character," in *Civilian Morale,* ed. Goodwin Watson (New York and Boston: Houghton Mifflin, 1942), pp. 71–91.

———, "Bali: The Value System of a Steady State," in *Social Structure, Studies Presented to A. R. Radcliffe-Brown,* ed. Meyer Fortes (Oxford: Clarendon Press, 1949), pp. 35–53.

———, *Steps to an Ecology of Mind* (New York: Chandler, 1972).

———, "Double Bind, 1969," in *Steps to an Ecology of Mind* (New York: Chandler, 1972), pp. 271–78.

Bateson, Gregory et al, "Toward a Theory of Schizophrenia," *Behavioral Science* 1 (1956): 251–64.

Bateson, Gregory and Mead, Margaret, *Balinese Character: A Photographic Analysis* (New York Academy of Sciences, 1942).

Bateson, Mary Catherine, *Our Own Metaphor: A Personal Account of a Conference on the Effects of Conscious Purpose on Human Adaptation* (New York: Knopf, 1972).

Benedict, Ruth, *Patterns of Culture* (Boston: Houghton Mifflin, 1934).

Benedict, Ruth, "Thai Culture and Behavior," unpublished wartime study dated September, 1943, Southeast Asia Program Data Paper no. 4, Department of Far Eastern Studies, Cornell University, 1952, pp. 44–48.

Bidyalankarana, Prince, "Rhyme Making and Singing in Rural Siam," *Journal of the Siam Society* 20 (1926): 101–27.

Campbell, J. G. D., *Siam in the Twentieth Century* (London: E. Arnold, 1902).

Erikson, Erik H., *Childhood and Society,* rev. ed. (New York: Norton, 1963).

Fortune, Reo F., *Sorcerers of Dobu* (London: George Routledge and Sons, 1932).

Gewertz, Deborah, "Economic Advantage and the Power of Submission in the Middle Sepik." Paper presented at the American Anthropological Association, 75th Annual Meeting, November 21, 1976. In press.

Gorer, Geoffrey, "Japanese Character, Structure and Propaganda, A Preliminary Survey," mimeographed (New York: Institute for Intercultural Studies, 1942).

———, *The American People* (New York: Norton, 1948).

———, "To See Ourselves," in *Exploring English Character* (London: The Cresset Press, 1955), pp. 278–304.

Hoyt, N. S., "Source Material: Types of Folklore Which Exist in Soviet Union," Archives of the American Museum of Natural History Project, Studies in Soviet Culture, 1947–1950.

Joffe, Natalie F., "Non-Reciprocity Among East European Jews," in *The Study of Culture at a Distance,* ed. Margaret Mead and Rhoda Métraux (Chicago: University of Chicago Press, 1953), pp. 386–89.

———, "The Dynamics of Benefice Among East European Jews," *Social Forces* 27 (1949): 238–47.

Kretschmer, Ernst, *Physique and Character,* 2nd rev. enl. ed. (New York: Harcourt, Brace, 1925).

Leites, Nathan. "Trends in Affectlessness." In *The Study of Culture at a Distance,* Margaret Mead and Rhoda Métraux, eds. (Chicago: University of Chicago Press, 1953), pp. 248–263.

Maclean, Paul D., "The Triune Brain," *Medical World News Review* 1, no. 2 (October, 1974): 55, 59, 60.

Mead, Margaret, *Social Organization of Manu'a,* Bernice P. Bishop Museum Bulletin 76 (Honolulu: Bishop Museum Press, 1930).

———, *Sex and Temperament* (New York: Morrow, 1935).

———, *And Keep Your Powder Dry* (New York: Morrow, 1942).

Mead, Margaret (with A. Murray Dyer), "It's Human Nature," *Education,* 65, no. 4 (December, 1944), 228–238.

———, "The Application of Anthropological Techniques to Cross-National Communication," *Transactions of the New York Academy of Sciences* ser. 2, vol. 9, no. 4 (New York, February, 1947): 133–52.

———, "A Case History in Cross-National Communications," in *The Communication of Ideas,* ed. Lyman Bryson (New York: Institute for Religion and Social Studies, 1948), pp. 209–29.

———, *Male and Female* (New York: Morrow, 1949).

———, *Soviet Attitudes Toward Authority* (New York: McGraw-Hill, 1951).

———, *An Anthropologist at Work: Writings of Ruth Benedict* (Boston: Houghton Mifflin, 1959).

———, "The Factor of Culture," in *The Selection of Personnel for Internationl Service,* ed. Mottram Torre (Geneva and New York: World Federation for Mental Health, 1963), pp. 3–22.

———, *Culture and Commitment* (Garden City: Natural History Press/Doubleday, 1970).

———, *Blackberry Winter: My Earlier Years* (New York: Morrow, 1972).

———, *Ruth Benedict* (New York and London: Columbia University Press, 1974).

———, "On Freud's View of Female Psychology," in *Women and Analysis,* ed. Jean Strouse (New York: Grossman, 1974), pp. 95–106.

———, "Why Do We Speak of Feminine Intuition?" *Anima* 1 (1975): 44–49.

———, "Sex Differences: Innate, Learned or Situational?" *The Quarterly Journal of the Library of Congress* 32 (1975b): 260–267.

Métraux, Rhoda, "A Note on the Spectator in French Culture," in *The Study of Culture at a Distance,* ed. Margaret Mead and Rhoda Métraux (Chicago: University of Chicago Press, 1953), pp. 390–96.

———, "Cherishing and Preserving: Sex Differences and the Life of the World." *The Quarterly Journal of the Library of Congress* 32 (1975): 270–273.

Métraux, Rhoda and Mead, Margaret, *Themes in French Culture* (Stanford: Stanford Univ. Press, 1954).

Murray, Margaret A., *The Witch Cult in Western Europe: A Study in Anthropology* (Oxford: Oxford Univ. Press, 1963).

Peyre, Henri, *Writers and Their Critics* (Ithaca, New York: Cornell Univ. Press, 1944).

Tiger, Lionel, *Men in Groups* (New York: Random House, 1969).

Young, Ernest, *The Kingdom of the Yellow Robe*, 2nd ed. (London: Constable, 1900).

Zborowski, Mark, *People In Pain* (San Francisco: Jossey-Bass, 1969).

Afterword

❂ ❂

GREGORY BATESON

Dear John:

When you first suggested this volume and undertook to put it together, I said, "Don't let it be a *Festschrift*," and we agreed that you would ask your authors rather for some work and thinking of theirs that might have developed out of or alongside some part of my work. You would ask not for praise or criticism, but for some original material of theirs. So let me thank them, and then become, myself, one of your authors. Rather than replying to the other authors, let me tell you where I stand today and what, for me, came out of all that work in New Guinea and Bali and, later, with schizophrenics and dolphins.

As you know, the difficulty was always to get people to approach the formal analysis of mind with a similar or even an open epistemology. Many people claim to have no epistemology and must just overcome this optimism. Only then can they approach the particular epistemology here proposed. In other words, *two* jumps are required of the reader, and of these the first is the more difficult. We all cling fast to the illusion that we are capable of direct perception, uncoded and not mediated by epistemology. The double bind hypothesis—i.e., the *mental* description of schizophrenia—was itself a contribution to epistemology, and to evaluate it was an exercise, if you please, in a sort of metaepistemology. Epistemology itself is becoming a recursive subject, a recursive study of recursiveness. So that anybody encountering the double bind hypothesis has the problem that epistemology was already changed by the double bind hypothesis, and the hypothesis itself therefore has to be approached with the modified way of thinking which the hypothesis had proposed.

I am sure that none of us in the 1950s realized how difficult this was. Indeed, we still did not realize that, if our hypothesis was even partly correct, it must also be important as a contribution to what I have sometimes called the "fundamentals"—our stock of "necessary" truths.

So what I have to do now is to tell you how, for me, an epistemology grew out of ethnographic observation and cybernetic theory, and how this epistemology determines not only double bind theory and all the thinking that has followed in the field of psychiatry but also affects evolutionary thinking and the whole body-mind problem.

I have to present here a description of an epistemology, and then I have to fit the double bind hypothesis and thoughts about evolution into that epistemology. In a word, I have to invite the reader to come in *backward* upon the whole business.

From time to time I get complaints that my writing is dense and hard to understand. It may comfort those who find the matter hard to understand if I tell them that I have driven myself, over the years, into a "place" where conventional dualistic statements of mind-body relations—the conventional dualisms of Darwinism, psychoanalysis, and theology—are absolutely unintelligible to me. It is becoming as difficult for me to understand dualists as it is for them to understand me. And I fear that it's not going to become easier, except by those others being slowly exercised in the art of thinking along those pathways that seem to me to be "straight." My friends in New Guinea, the Iatmul, whose language and culture I studied, used to say, "But our language is so easy. We just talk."

So in writing about evolution—in trying to write about it—a second book has started to appear. It became necessary to tell the reader a number of very elementary (as it seemed to me) things which he certainly ought to have learned in high school but which Anglo-Saxons certainly do not learn in high school. This book, budded from the first, larger book, I called, tentatively, *What Every Schoolboy Knows,* an ironic quote from Lord Macaulay. What the good gentleman really said was, "Every schoolboy knows who imprisoned Montezuma and who strangled Atahualpa."

Let me start by trying to characterize my epistemology as it has grown under my hands, with some notable influence from other people.

First, it is a branch of natural history. It was McCulloch who, for me, pulled epistemology down out of the realms of abstract philosophy into the much more simple realm of natural history. This was dramatically done in the paper by McCulloch and his friends entitled "What the Frog's Eye Told the Frog's Brain." In that paper he showed that any answer to the question "How can a frog know anything?" would be delimited by the sensory machinery of the frog; and that the sensory machinery of the frog could, indeed, be investigated by experimental and other means. It turned out that the frog could only receive news of such moving objects as subtended less than ten degrees at the eye. All else was invisible and produced no impulses on the optic nerve. From this paper it followed that, to understand human beings, even at a very elementary level, you had to know the limitations of their sensory input.

And that matter became part of my experience when I went through the experiments of Adelbert Ames, Jr. I discovered that when I see something, or hear a sound, or taste, it is my brain, or perhaps I should better say "mind"—it is I who create an image in the modality of the appropriate sense organ. My image is my aggregation and organization of information about the perceived object, aggregated and integrated by me according to rules of which I am totally unconscious. I can, thanks to Ames, know *about* these rules; but I cannot be conscious of the process of their working.

Ames showed me that I (and you), looking through our eyes, *create,* out of showers of impulses on the optic nerve, images of the perceived that appear to be three-dimensional images. I "see" an image *in depth.* But the way in which that image is given depth depends upon essentially Euclidian arguments within the brain and of which the perceiver is unconscious. It is as if the perceiver knew the premises of parallax and created his image in accordance with those rules, never letting himself know at any conscious level that he has applied the rules of parallax to the shower of impulses. Indeed, the whole process, including the shower of impulses itself, is a totally unconscious business.

It seems to be a universal feature of human perception, a feature of the underpinning of human epistemology, that the perceiver shall perceive only the product of his perceiving act. He shall not perceive the means by which that product was created. The product itself is a sort of work of art.

But along with this detached natural history, in which I, as an epistemology, describe the frog or myself—along with that natural history goes a curious and unexpected addition. Now that we have pulled epistemology down from philosophy and made it a branch of natural history, it becomes necessarily a *normative* branch of natural history. This study is normative in the sense that it will chide us when we ignore its strictures and regularities. One had not expected that natural history could be normative, but indeed, the epistemology which I am building for you is normative in two almost synonymous ways. It can be wrong, or I can be wrong about it. And either of those two sorts of error becomes itself part of any epistemology in which it occurs. Any error will propose pathology. (But I *am* the epistemology.)

Take the statement in a previous paragraph, The organism builds images in depth out of the shower of impulses brought to the brain by the optic nerve. It is possible that this statement is incorrect, that future scientific study of the act of perception may show that this is not so, or that its syntax is inappropriate. That is what I mean by being in error in the first way. And the second way of possible error would be to believe that the images that I see are in fact that which I am looking at, that my mental map *is* the external territory. (But we wander off into philosophy if we ask, "Is there *really* a territory?")

And then there is the fact that the epistemology I am building is *monistic*. Applying Occam's Razor, I decline to pay attention to notions—which others assert to be subjectively supported—that mind or soul is somehow separable from body and from matter. On the other hand, it is absolutely necessary, of course, that my epistemology shall allow for the natural history fact that, indeed, many human beings of many different cultures have the belief that the mind is indeed separable from the body. Their epistemology is either dualistic or pluralistic. In other words, in this normative natural history called epistemology there must be a study of errors, and evidently certain sorts of error are predictably common. If you look over the whole span of my work, starting with the notion of schismogenesis, or starting even with the patterns in partridge feathers and going from that to schismogenesis in New Guinea to end linkage in national character, to the double bind and to the material we got from the porpoises, you will see that up to a certain date my language of report is *dualistic*.

The double bind work was for me a documentation of the idea that mind is a necessary explanatory principle. Simple nineteenth-century materialism will not accept any hierarchy of ideas or differences. The world of mindlessness, the Pleroma, contains no *names*, no *classes*.

It is here that I have always in my thinking followed Samuel Butler in his criticisms of Darwinian evolution. It always seems to me that the Darwinian phrasings were an effort to exclude mind. And indeed that materialism in general was an effort to exclude mind. And therefore, since materialism is rather barren, it was hardly surprising to me as an epistemological naturalist to note that physicists, from William Crookes onward, have been prone to go to mediums and other tricksters. They needed solace in their materialism.

But the matter was always difficult. I could not tolerate the dualism seriously, and yet I knew that the narrow materialistic statement was a gross oversimplification of the biological world. The solution came when I was preparing the Korzybski Lecture, when I suddenly realized that of course the bridge between map and territory is *difference*. It is only *news of difference* that can get from the territory to the map, and this fact is the basic epistemological statement about the relationship between all reality out there and all perception in here: that the bridge must always be in the form of difference. Difference, out there, precipitates coded or corresponding difference in the aggregate of differentiation which we call the organism's mind. And that mind is immanent in matter, which is partly inside the body—but also partly "outside," e.g., in the form of records, traces, and perceptibles.

Difference, you see, is just sufficiently away from the grossly materialistic and quantitative world so that mind, dealing in difference, will always be intangible, will always deal in intangibles, and will always have certain limitations because it can never encounter with Immanuel Kant called the *Ding an Sich,* the thing in itself. It can only encounter news of boundaries—news of the contexts of difference.

It is worthwhile to list several points about "difference" here.

1. A difference is not material and cannot be localized. If this apple is different from that egg, the difference does not lie in the apple or in the egg, or in the space between them. To locate difference, i.e., to delimit the context or interface, would be to posit a world incapable of change. Zeno's famous arrow could never move from a position "here" in this context to a position "there" in the next context.

2. Difference cannot be placed in time. The egg can be sent to Alaska or can be destroyed, and still the difference remains. Or is it only the news of the difference that remains? Or is the

difference ever anything but news? With a million differences between the egg and the apple, only those become information that make a difference.

3. Difference is not a quantity. It is dimensionless and, for sense organs, digital. It is delimited by threshold.

4. Those differences, or news of differences, which are information, must not be confused with "energy." The latter is a quantity with physical dimensions (Mass × the square of a Velocity). It is perfectly clear that information does not have dimensions of this kind;* and that information travels, usually, where energy already is. That is, the recipient, the organism receiving information—or the end organ or the neuron—is already energized from its metabolism, so that, for example, the impulse can travel along the nerve, not driven by the energy, but finding energy ready to undergo degradation at every point of the travel. The energy is there in advance of the information or the response. This distinction between information and energy becomes conspicuous whenever that which does not happen triggers response in an organism. I commonly tell my classes that if they don't fill in their income tax forms the Internal Revenue people will respond to the difference between the forms which they don't fill in and the forms which they might have filled in. Or your aunt, if you don't write her a letter, will respond to the difference between the letter you do not write and the letter you might have written. A tick on the twig of a tree waits for the smell of butyric acid that would mean "mammal in the neighborhood." When he smells the butyric acid, he will fall from the tree. But if he stays long enough on the tree and there is no butyric acid, he will fall from the tree anyway and go to climb up another one. He can respond to the "fact" that something does not happen.

5. Last in regard to information, and the identity between information and news of difference, I want to give a sort of special honor to Gustav Fechner, who in the 1840s got a whiff of this enormously powerful idea. It drove him almost mad,

* But, of course, a *difference* in energy (not itself of the dimensions of energy) can generate news of difference.

but he is still remembered and his name is still carried in the Weber-Fechner Law. He must have been an extraordinarily gifted man, and a very strange one.

To continue my sketch of the epistemology that grew out of my work, the next point is recursiveness. Here there seem to be two species of recursiveness, of somewhat different nature, of which the first goes back to Norbert Wiener and is well known, the "feedback" that is perhaps the best-known feature of the whole cybernetic syndrome. The point is that self-corrective and quasi purposive systems necessarily and always have the characteristic that causal trains within the system are themselves circular. Such causal trains, when independently energized, are either self-corrective or runaway systems. In the wider epistemology, it seems that, necessarily, a causal train either in some sense dies out as it spreads through the universe, or returns to the point from which it started. In the first case there is no question of its survival. In the second case, by returning to the place from which it started, a subsystem is established which, for greater or less length of time, will necessarily survive.

The second type of recursiveness has been proposed by Varela and Maturana. These mathematicians discuss the case in which some property of a *whole* is fed back into the system, producing a somewhat different type of recursiveness, for which Varela has worked out the formalisms. We live in a universe in which causal trains endure, survive through time, only if they are recursive. They "survive"—i.e., literally *live upon themselves*—and some survive longer than others.

If our explanations or our understanding of the universe is in some sense to match that universe, or model it, and if the universe is recursive, then our explanations and our logics must also be fundamentally recursive.

And finally there is the somewhat disputed area of "levels." For me the double bind, among other things, as a phenomenon of natural history, is strong evidence that, at least in the natural history aspects of epistemology, we encounter phenomena that are generated by organisms whose epistemology is, for better or for worse, structured in hierarchic form. It seems to me very clear and even expectable that end organs can receive only news of difference. Each receives difference and creates news of difference; and, of course, this proposes the possibility of differences between differences, and differences that are differently effective or differently meaningful according to the network within which they exist. This is the path toward an epistemology of gestalt psychology, and this clumping of news of difference becomes especially true of the mind when it, in its characteristic natural history, evolves language and faces the circumstance that the name is not the thing named, and the name of the name is not the name. This is the area in which I've worked very considerably in constructing a hypothetical hierarchy of species of learning.

These four components, then, give you the beginnings of a sketch of an epistemology:

1. That message events are activated by difference.
2. That information travels in pathways and systems that are collaterally energized (with a few exceptions where the energy itself in some form, perhaps a light, a temperature, or a motion, *is* the traveling information). The separation of energy is made clear in a very large number of cases in which the difference is fundamentally a difference between zero and one. In such cases, "zero-not-one" can be the message, which differs from "one-not-zero."
3. A special sort of holism is generated by feedback and recursiveness.
4. That mind operates with hierarchies and networks of difference to create *gestalten.*

I want to make clear that there are a number of very important statements that are not made in this sketch of an epistemology and whose absence is an important characteristic. I said above that, as I see it and believe it, the universe and any description of it is monistic; and this would imply a certain continuity of the entire world of information. But there is a very strong tendency in Western thinking (perhaps in all human thinking) to think and talk as if the world were made up of separable parts.

All peoples of the world, I believe, certainly all existing peoples, have something like language and, so far as I can understand the talk of linguists, it seems that all languages depend upon a particulate representation of the universe. All languages have something like nouns and verbs, isolating objects, entities, events, and abstractions. In whatever way you phrase it, "difference" will always propose delimitations and boundaries. If our means of *describing* the world arises out of notions of difference (or what G. Spencer Brown's *Laws of Form* calls "distinction" and "indication"), then our picture of the universe will necessarily be particulate. It becomes an act of faith to distrust language and to believe in monism. Of necessity we shall still split our descriptions when we talk about the universe. But there may be better and worse ways of doing this splitting of the universe into nameable parts.

Finally, let me try to give you an idea of what it felt like, or what sort of difference it made, for me to view the world in terms of the epistemology that I have described to you, instead of viewing it as I used to and as I believe most people always do.

First of all, let me stress what happens when one becomes aware that there is much that is our own contribution to our own perception. Of course I am no more aware of the processes of my own perception than anybody else is. But I am aware that there are such processes, and this awareness means that when I look out through my eyes and see the redwoods or the yellow flowering acacia of California roadsides, I know that I am doing all sorts of things to my percept in order to make sense of that percept. Of course I always did this, and everybody does it. We work hard to make sense, according to our epistemology, of the world which we think we see.

Whoever creates an image of an object does so in depth, using various cues for that creation, as I have already said in discussing the Ames experiments. But most people are not aware that they do this, and as you become aware that you are doing it, you become in a curious way much closer to the world around you. The word "objective" becomes, of course, quite quietly obsolete; and at the same time the word "subjective," which normally confines "you" within your skin, disappears as well. It is, I think, the debunking of the objective that is the important change. The world is no longer "out there" in quite the same way that it used to seem to be. Without being fully conscious or thinking about it all the time, I still know all the time that my images—especially the visual, but also auditory, gustatory, pain, and fatigue—I know the images are "mine" and that I am responsible for these images in a quite peculiar way. It is as if they are all in some degree hallucinated, as indeed they partly are. The shower of impulses coming in over the optic nerve surely contains no picture. The picture is to be developed, to be created, by the intertwining of all these neural messages. And the brain that can do this must be pretty smart. It's my brain. But everybody's brain—any mammalian brain—can do it, I guess.

I have the use of the information that that which I see, the images, or that which I feel as pain, the prick of a pin, or the ache of a tired muscle—for these, too, are images created in their respective modes—that all this is neither objective truth nor is it all hallucination. There is a combining or marriage between an objectivity that is *passive* to the outside world and a creative subjectivity, neither pure solipsism nor its opposite.

Consider for a moment the phrase, *the opposite of solipsism.* In solipsism, you are ultimately isolated and alone, isolated by the premise "I make it all up." But at the other extreme, the opposite of solipsism, you would cease to exist, becoming nothing but a metaphoric feather blown by the winds of external "reality." (But in that region there are no metaphors!) Somewhere between these two is a region where you are partly blown by the winds of reality and partly an artist creating a composite out of the inner and outer events.

A smoke ring is, literally and etymologically, introverted. It is endlessly turning upon itself, a torus, a doughnut, spinning on the axis of the circular cylinder that is the doughnut. And this turning upon its own in-turned axis is what gives separable existence to the smoke ring. It is, after all, made of nothing but air marked with a little smoke. It is of the same substance as its "environment." But it has duration and location and a certain degree of separation by virtue of its in-turned motion. In a sense, the smoke ring stands as a very primitive, oversimplified paradigm for all recursive systems that contain the beginnings of self-reference, or, shall we say, selfhood.

But if you ask me, "Do you feel like a smoke ring all the time?" of course my answer is no. Only at very brief moments, in flashes of awareness, am I that realistic. Most of the time I still see the world, feel it, the way I always did. Only at certain moments am I aware of my own introversion. But these are enlightening moments that demonstrate the irrelevance of intervening states.

And as I try to tell you about this, lines from Robert Browning's "Grammarian's Funeral" keep coming to mind.

> Yea, this in him was the peculiar grace . . .
> That before living he learned how to live.

Or again,

> He settled *Hoti's* business—let it be!—
> Properly based *Oun*—
> Gave us the doctrine of the enclitic *De*,
> Dead from the waist down.

And again, there is the misquotation that is going the rounds today,

> A man's reach should exceed his grasp,
> Or what's a meta for?

I'm afraid this American generation has mostly forgotten "The Grammarian's Funeral" with its strange combination of awe and contempt.

Imagine, for a moment, that the grammarian was neither an adventurous explorer, breaking through into realms previously unexplored, nor an intellectual, withdrawn from warm humanity into a cold but safe realm. Imagine that he was neither of these, but merely a human being rediscovering what every other human being and perhaps every dog—always instinctively and unconsciously—knew: that the dualisms of mind and body, of mind and matter, and of God and world are all somehow faked up. He would be terribly alone. He might invent something like the epistemology I have been trying to describe, emerging from the repressed state, which Freud called "latency," into a more-or-less distorted rediscovery of that which had been hidden. Perhaps all exploration of the world of ideas is only a searching for a rediscovery, and perhaps it is such rediscovery of the latent that defines us as "human," "conscious," and "twice born." But if this be so, then we all must sometimes hear St. Paul's "voice" echoing down the ages: "It is hard for thee to kick against the pricks."

I am suggesting to you that all the multiple insults, the double binds and invasions that we all experience in life, the impact (to use an inappropriate physical word) whereby experience corrupts our epistemology, challenging the core of our existence, and thereby seducing us into a false cult of the ego—what I am suggesting is that the process whereby double binds and other traumas teach us a false epistemology is already well advanced in most occidentals and perhaps most orientals, and that those whom we call "schizophrenics" are those in whom the endless kicking against the pricks has become intolerable.

GREGORY

CURRICULUM VITAE
Gregory Bateson

Born May 9, 1904, Grantchester, England, son of William Bateson, F.R.S. Naturalized U.S. citizen February 7, 1956.

1917–21 Student, Charterhouse, England.

1922–26 Cambridge University. Entrance Scholar St. John's College, 1922, Foundation Scholar, 1924; Natural Science Tripos, first class honors, 1924. Anthropologist Tripos, first class honors, 1926.

B.A., 1925, Natural Science.

M.A., 1930 Anthropology.

1927–29 Anthony Wilkin Student of Cambridge University. The period of this studentship was spent in anthropological fieldwork in New Britain and New Guinea.

1931–37 Fellow of St. John's College, Cambridge.

1931–33, Anthropological fieldwork, New Guinea, financed jointly by Fellowship and by the Royal Society.

1934, Visit to the United States. Lectured at Columbia and Chicago.

1936, Married Margaret Mead (divorced, 1950). One daughter.

1936–38, Anthropological fieldwork, Bali.

1938–39 Anthropological fieldwork, New Guinea.

1939 Brief fieldwork, Bali.

1940 Entered the United States as a resident.

1941 Film analysis with the Museum of Modern Art, New York City.

1942–45 Office of Strategic Services of the U.S. Government. Overseas in Ceylon, India, Burma, and China.

1946–47 Visiting Professor, New School for Social Research, New York.

1947–48 Visiting Professor, Harvard University, Cambridge, Massachusetts.

1947 Guggenheim Fellow.

1948–49 University of California Medical School. Research Associate with Dr. Jurgen Ruesch.

1949–to date Ethnologist at Veteran's Administration Hospital, Palo Alto, California. Engaged in teaching and research on the borderline fields of anthropology, psychiatry, and cybernetics.

1951–to date Part-time Visiting Professor, Stanford University, in the Department of Anthropology.

1952–54 Director, Research Project on the Role of the Paradoxes of Abstraction in Communication, under a grant from the Rockefeller Foundation.

1954–59 Director, Research Project on Schizophrenic Communication, under a grant from the Josiah Macy, Jr., Foundation.

1959–62 Principal Investigator, Research in Family Psychotherapy, under a grant from the Foundation's Fund for Research in Psychiatry.

Part-time Professor, California School of Fine Arts, San Francisco, California.

1961 Frieda Fromm-Reichmann Award for research in schizophrenia.

1963–64 Associate Director, Communication Research Institute, St. Thomas, U.S. Virgin Islands.

1964 Career Development Award, National Institute of Mental Health.

1965 Associate Director for Research, Oceanic Institute, Waimanalo, Hawaii.

1972–to date Visiting Professor, University of California at Santa Cruz, Santa Cruz, California.

1976 Member, Board of Regents, University of California.

BIBLIOGRAPHY
of the Works of Gregory Bateson

Balinese Character: A Photographic Analysis. Special Publications of the New York Academy of Sciences, vol. 2. New York: New York Academy of Sciences, 1942. With Margaret Mead.

Communication: The Social Matrix of Psychiatry. New York: W. W. Norton, 1951. With Jurgen Ruesch.

Naven: A Survey of the Problems Suggested by a Composite Picture of the Culture of a New Guinea Tribe Drawn from Three Points of View. Cambridge: Cambridge Univ. Press, 1936. 2d ed., with "Epilogue 1958." Stanford: Stanford Univ. Press, 1965.

Perceval's Narrative: A Patient's Account of His Psychosis, 1830–1832, by John Perceval. Edited with an Introduction by Gregory Bateson. Stanford: Stanford Univ. Press, 1961.

Steps to An Ecology of Mind: Collected Essays in Anthropology, Psychiatry, Evolution, and Epistemology. New York: Ballantine Books, 1972.